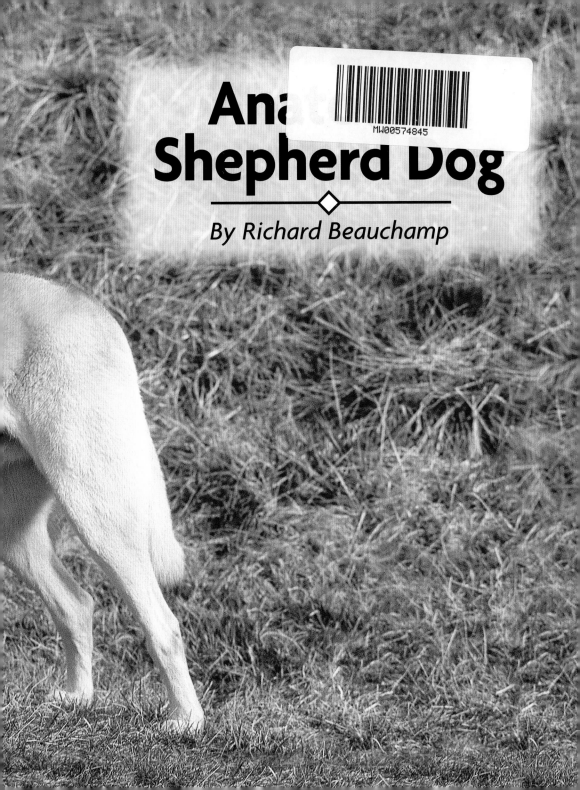

Ana[t]
Shepherd Dog

By Richard Beauchamp

Contents

KENNEL CLUB BOOKS® ANATOLIAN SHEPHERD DOG

ISBN: 1-59378-347-7

Copyright © 2003, **2006** • Kennel Club Books, LLC
308 Main Street, Allenhurst, NJ 07711 USA
Cover Design Patented: US 6,435,559 B2 • Printed in South Korea

Photography by Isabelle Français and Carol Ann Johnson
with additional photographs by:

Norvia Behling, T. J. Calhoun, Carolina Biological Supply, David Dalton, Doskocil, James Hayden-Yoav, James R. Hayden, RBP, Lynette Hodge, Bill Jonas, Dwight R. Kuhn, Dr. Dennis Kunkel, Mikki Pet Products, Phototake, Jean Claude Revy, Dr. Andrew Spielman and Alice van Kempen.

Illustrations by Patricia Peters.

The publisher would like to thank all of the owners of the dogs featured in this book, including Mrs. Pat & Miss "Shell" Broadhead, Louise V. Emanuel and Charles M. Zimmerman.

A section from "Las Meninas" (The Maids of Honor), a famous painting by Diego Velazquez de Silva. The figures in the painting are caught in snapshot fashion in typical Velazquez style. The dog at the children's feet, though not identified by breed, certainly resembles the Anatolian Shepherd. Painted in 1656, the original is in the Philip IV collection at the Prado Museum in Madrid, Spain.

HISTORY OF THE
ANATOLIAN
SHEPHERD DOG

ANCIENT HISTORY OF DOGS

There are well beyond 300 separate and distinct breeds of dog that are officially recognized today by the respective pure-bred dog registries of the world. What comes as a surprise to many is that all breeds, regardless of size, shape or color, trace back to a single common ancestor. And, what may be even more important in the overall scheme of things, our search reveals that the development of the dog bears a striking parallel to the development of humankind itself.

In order to fully understand why any given breed looks and acts as it does, you must go back to the dawn of civilization—a time when humankind's major pursuit in life was simply that of survival. Providing food for himself and his family and protecting the members of the tribe from danger were about as much as early man could handle.

During this time, early man undoubtedly saw his own survival efforts reflected in the habits of one of the beasts of the forest—a beast that made ever-increasing overtures at coexistence. That

GENUS *CANIS*

Dogs and wolves are members of the genus *Canis*. Wolves are known scientifically as *Canis lupus* while dogs are known as *Canis domesticus*. Dogs and wolves are known to interbreed. The term "canine" derives from the Latin-derived word *Canis*. The term "dog" has no scientific basis but has been used for thousands of years. The origin of the word "dog" has never been authoritatively ascertained.

beast was none other than *Canis lupus*—the wolf. Thus, a relationship based purely upon the need to survive had begun. The ages themselves, however, would show that this was a kinship that would prove far more beneficial to humankind than anyone could ever have imagined.

Wolf families had already developed a cooperative and efficient system of hunting the food they needed for survival. Man was not only able to emulate some of these techniques but, as time passed, he found he was also able to employ the help of the wolves themselves in capturing the animals that would constitute a good part of the human diet. In turn, wolves saw a source of easily secured food in man's discards and, moving in closer and closer, the more cooperative wolves found that they had increasingly less to fear of man. The association grew from there.

"MAN'S BEST FRIEND" ARRIVES

The road from wolf-in-the-wild to "man's best friend"—*Canis familiaris*—is as long and fascinating as it is fraught with widely varying explanations. There seems to be universal agreement, however, that the wolves able to assist man in satisfying the unending human need for food were the most highly prized.

In *The Natural History of Dogs*, a study of the development of dog breeds, authors Richard and Alice Feinnes classify most dogs as having descended from one of four major groups. Each of these groups traces back to separate and distinct branches of the wolf family. The groups are known as the Dingo Group, the Greyhound Group, the Northern Group and the Mastiff Group.

The Dingo Group traces its origin to the Asian Wolf (*Canis lupus pallipes*). Two well-known examples of the Dingo Group are the Basenji and, through the admixture of several European breeds, the Rhodesian Ridgeback.

The Greyhound Group descends from a coursing-type relative of the Asian Wolf. The group includes all those dogs that hunt by sight and are capable of great speed. The Greyhound itself, the Afghan Hound, the Borzoi and Irish Wolfhound are all examples of this group and are known as the coursing breeds or sight-hounds. They are not true hounds in that they do not hunt by scent.

The Northern Group (also Arctic or Nordic Group) of dogs descends directly from the rugged Northern Wolf (*Canis lupus*). Included in the many breeds of this group are the Alaskan Malamute, Chow Chow, German Shepherd and the much smaller Welsh Corgis, and the Spitz-type dogs.

The fourth classification, and the one we take particular interest in here, is the Mastiff Group, which owes its primary heritage to the rugged Woolly Tibetan Wolf (*Canis lupus chanco* or *laniger*). The great diversity of the dogs included in this group indicates that they are not entirely of pure blood in that the specific breeds included have characteristics that reveal that they have been influenced by descendants of the other three groups. This widely divergent group is known to include many breeds we now classify as Sporting Dogs, such as the (scent) hounds, as well as the guard/protection and flock-guardian dogs.

It is the ingenuity of man that deserves full credit for the

selective process that produced dogs who excelled in some but not all of the traits that had been passed down from their lupine ancestors. The undesirable charac-teristics that could have been inherited were practically nullified. A perfect example of this will be seen in how the wolf's territorial instinct, communal spirit and bravery are reflected in the character and working ability of the Great Pyrenees (known in England as the Pyrenean Mountain Dog)—thought to be one of the oldest pure-bred breeds in the world.

As humankind moved out of the caves and developed a more sophisticated and complex lifestyle, man found he could produce animals that could suit his specific needs from these descendants of the wolf. More often than not, this selective process was shaped by how and where man lived.

The wolves that had been accustomed to herding, separating and killing their prey in the forest were selectively bred to retain their rugged constitution and their ability to round up their prey, but the prey instinct itself was, for all intents and purposes, eliminated. From still other descendants of the original wolf stock, man eliminated both the prey and herding instincts in favor of developing their communal and protective qualities. They did so

The Great Pyrenees, or Pyrenean Mountain Dog, known for strong character and working ability, is considered to be one of the oldest breeds of dog.

in order to ensure the safety of their domesticated livestock.

It is at about this point in history that we can stop calling wolves "wolves" and start referring to them as *Canis familiaris* or, for the non-Latin-speaking among us, "dogs." Particular characteristics were prized and inbreeding practices were used both to intensify the desired characteristics and eliminate those that opposed the efficiency of the dogs.

THE ANATOLIAN PLATEAU

When the Mongoloid peoples migrated westward into Europe,

ANCESTORS OF OUR ANATOLIANS

Throughout history, there have been written reports of huge mastiff-type dogs that have existed since Babylonian times. The dogs were used to guard flocks for the shepherds, who eked out their meager existence from the Anatolian Plateau. The extremely swift and powerful dogs also were known to be capable of running down lions and assisting as war dogs by pulling men down from their horses. It is believed that these dogs were the Anatolian Shepherd Dogs' ancient ancestors.

Another of the European mountain-patrolling breeds is the Maremmani or Maremma Sheepdog of Italy.

PROTECTOR OF CHILDREN

The highly developed guarding sense of the Anatolian Shepherd Dog was put to use by Turkish women when their dogs had no flock to protect. When called upon to work in the fields, the women would sometimes tie one end of a rope around their young children's waists and the other end to their Anatolian's collar. The women could then go about their work in the field with no worry as to the safety of their children.

their dogs, Mastiff-type descendants of the rugged Woolly Tibetan Wolf, went with them. The migrants dispersed themselves throughout the main mountain ranges of Europe, where environment and the specific needs of the people developed their dogs into separate and distinct types.

There are no written records to indicate what blood may have been introduced and combined with these early canine immigrants to produce the flock guardians that followed. We do know, however, that these dogs

One of the flock guardian breeds from Hungary, the Kuvasz.

The Hungarian Komondor, with its distinctive corded coat, is a rare shepherding breed.

patrolled the flocks throughout the European continent's mountain ranges, each in his own distinctive way. Among them we find the Hungarian Komondor of the Caucasus mountains, the Leonberger of Germany, the Kuvasz of Hungary, the Maremmani of the Italian Alps, the Great Pyrenees of France's Pyrenean range and, of course, the magnificent dogs that lived and worked along Turkey's Anatolian Plateau, the Anatolian Shepherd Dog.

We also know, that such a dog has patrolled the inhospitable Anatolian Plateau of central Turkey for several thousand years. Little has changed about the dog, as can be witnessed in the first evidence of the breed depicted on bas-reliefs that can be viewed in the Assyrian Room of the British Museum. These accurate portrayals document the existence of the dog now known as the Anatolian Shepherd Dog as far back as 3,000 years.

The Anatolian Plateau extends from the Black to the Mediterranean Seas—the area the Greeks and Romans called Asia, later to become known as Asia Minor to distinguish it from the continent of Asia. The dogs that watched over the flocks there had to be tough in every aspect—physically hardy and totally impervious to every element nature inflicted upon them.

Torrid summer months brought triple-digit temperatures

that plummeted to 60 degrees below 0 through the winter months. And then, above all, the dog had to be brave, strong and fierce enough to fight off any threat to the flocks, whether predators arrived singly or in packs.

Thus was developed a large dog of weather-proof coat with strong feet and legs that could withstand rocky and frozen terrain as well as blistering sand. These were not pets or companions. Their value to the herdsmen was in their ability to save the stock from predators. No special care was given the dogs and they had to get by on the most Spartan of rations. Responding to any temptation to bring down one of the animals that they guarded to satisfy their need for sustenance meant instant death for the dog.

Turkish herdsmen called these dogs *Coban Kopegi*, which is simply translated to mean "Shepherd's Dog." As important as the dogs were to the safety and well-being of their herds, dogs were viewed as "unclean," as is common in many Moslem countries, and were accorded little care beyond that which was necessary to keep them alive for guard duty.

One can only wonder at the little regard these amazingly brave and versatile dogs were afforded by their owners. In addition to their courage, the dogs had to be capable of performing the most subtle and complex duties. The dogs lived almost entirely on their own, interacting with the shepherds only for their minimum basic necessities. They worked, slept, ate and traveled with the sheep and goats and, for all intents and purposes, were accepted as members of the flock. Lacking direction, the dogs themselves were called upon to make decisions necessary to

A fine representative of today's Anatolian Shepherd Dog.

Today's pet Anatolians are more likely to keep watch over the backyard than an unruly flock, but guarding instincts are still at the fore of the breed's temperament.

ensure the well-being of their flocks.

When not actually sleeping among their wards, these shepherd dogs would be found on a bluff just above the flock, where not a single animal could escape their gaze. When the dogs moved about, they did so slowly and quietly to avoid exciting the flock and throwing them into panic and stampede. When a predator appeared, however, the placid demeanor of the Anatolian Shepherd Dog disappeared. The gentle flock guardian became a raging and aggressive power-house, strong enough to bring down the fiercest adversary.

ANATOLIAN EXPORTS

With these credentials, it comes as no surprise that eventually the dogs would capture the attention of foreign visitors. It is believed the first Anatolian Shepherd Dogs to leave Turkey went to the United States as early as the 1930s when the first dogs were given to the United States Department of Agriculture (USDA) by the Turkish government. During the 1950s, Dr. Rodney Young, the archeologist responsible for the digs at the ancient Turkish city of Gordium (birthplace of the King Midas and Gordian Knot legends), also exported Anatolian Shepherd Dogs to his home in the US.

No active breeding program was initiated in the United States,

SOUND BY NATURE

Over the past several thousand years, the Anatolian Shepherd Dog has had absolutely no reason for existence other than to work on behalf of his flock master. Thus, no quarter has been given either by Nature or man in the area of unsoundness. Because of this ruthless culling, few hereditary defects exist in Turkish-bred Anatolians or in their direct descendants.

however, until 1970, when Lt. Robert C. Ballard, USN, who had been stationed in Ankara, Turkey, returned to the US with his imports "Zorba" and "Peki" and produced the first recorded American-bred litter of Anatolian Shepherd pups. The year 1970

SPIKED COLLARS

The spiked iron collars that one sees in pictures of working and guard dogs of many breeds are entirely misunderstood by most observers. They are not an offensive aid as some believe. The purpose of the collars, and the reason that Anatolian Shepherd Dogs living in Turkey are equipped with them, is for the sole purpose of protecting the dog's neck and throat from the attack of predators.

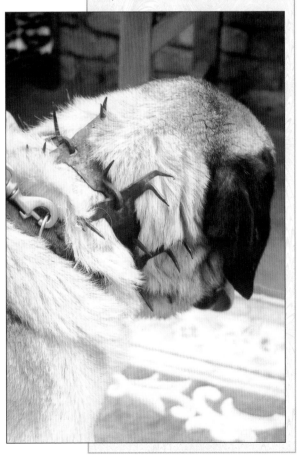

also saw the founding of the national breed club, the Anatolian Shepherd Dog Club of America (ASDCA).

In 1965, Anatolian Shepherds were exported to England. They were recorded by the The Kennel Club there as "Anatolian Sheepdogs," later to be renamed "Anatolian Karabash" and then finally, in 1983, "Anatolian Shepherd Dogs."

The ASDCA in the US met with a stumbling block in its quest for AKC recognition caused by a group that believed each of the Anatolian's several colors represented separate and distinct breeds. This situation caused great concern with the American Kennel Club as it had with The Kennel Club in England and was, in truth, what had created the periodic change of names with the organization.

It should be noted here that the tan dogs with black noses and ears are referred to as *Karabas* in Turkey. The English translation is "Karabash," meaning "black head." *Akbas* (English translation "Akbash" or "white head") describes the all-white dog in Turkish.

OFFICIAL BREED NAME

The entire matter of name and color was settled in 1983 by The Kennel Club in England. After years of hearings and what is said to have been thousands of pages

Today all colors are accepted in the Anatolian breed. This dog's black markings are typical of what is called *Karabas* in Turkey, the breed's homeland.

of testimony, a geneticist appointed by the organization testified that Karabas/Karabash and Akbas/Akbash were simply color descriptions and that using those terms to indicate distinct breeds was incorrect, regrettable and no longer valid—the breed's name was officially established as Anatolian Shepherd Dog. The name was also adopted by the American Kennel Club and by the Fédération Internationale Cynologique when it granted the breed full eligibility for international championship status.

The Anatolian Shepherd Dog Club of Great Britain was founded in 1979, setting preservation of the distinctive qualities of this centuries-old breed as its goal. The organization has a strict code of ethics regarding breeding and the main aim of the club is to promote and preserve the breed in all of its naturally occurring coat colors and textures while at the same time ensuring stable temperament and physical soundness.

The Anatolian Shepherd is a large dog that requires love, companionship, a proper diet and adequate space and time for exercise. Are you able to supply these needs? If not, you should not acquire an Anatolian.

CHARACTERISTICS OF THE
ANATOLIAN SHEPHERD DOG

ARE YOU READY FOR AN ANATOLIAN?

It would be hard for an observer who had never seen a full-grown Anatolian Shepherd Dog to guess that the stocky little youngsters playing in a whelping box could grow up to be such imposing adults. The little Anatolian puppy with his floppy ears, oversized feet and inquisitive expression gives little hint of things to come. However, their beguiling appearance as baby puppies are no more indicative of things to come than is their diminutive size.

In the case of the Anatolian Shepherd puppy, what you see is most definitely *not* what you will get. For this very reason, the person who anticipates owning an Anatolian must give serious thought to the final decision. All puppies are charming and, in most cases, even cuddly. Anatolian puppies are certainly no exception. You must remember, however, that puppies are living, breathing and very adventurous little creatures that will depend entirely upon their human owners

for everything once they leave their mother and littermates behind. And, in the case of an Anatolian, the end result may be more of an undertaking than the average person might be prepared for.

Careful consideration is appropriate regardless of any breed you might be thinking about bringing into your household. But beyond that, there are special considerations for those who might be thinking about the Anatolian as their first or even next dog.

As his history tells us, the Anatolian is a flock guardian and the absence of a flock makes the Anatolian no less a guardian, a job he performs at all costs! Centuries have been invested in cultivating and developing the breed's protective characteristics, and you must not delude yourself for a minute that you will be able to change that heritage. The Anatolian's entire genetic structure demands that he puts to use the very reason for which the breed was established and perpetuated. His well-being depends upon his being given the opportunity to exercise the mental and physical characteristics that he has inherited.

If given no flock to guard, the Anatolian Shepherd will protect you, your children, your property and any and every living thing that might be included in the territory over which he presides.

Given these opportunities, and given the guidelines by which his conduct is governed, the puppy you bring home will develop into a well-behaved and devoted companion whose loyalty could not possibly be surpassed by any other breed of dog.

Without an owner to set the rules, the Anatolian puppy can become an overbearing adolescent who grows into a domineering and aggressive adult that will make you regret ever having even considered dog ownership. Is the dog being impossible and incorrigible? No! The dog is simply following his nature, which demands that he put his incomparable abilities to good use. He believes that you have denied him this opportunity and failed in your responsibility to show him how you want this done.

Failure to think ahead and understand the amount of time and readjustment dog ownership involves is one of the primary reasons that there are so many abandoned canines that end their lives in animal shelters. Buying a dog, especially an Anatolian Shepherd Dog, before you are absolutely sure you want to make that commitment can be a serious mistake.

Before a person decides to buy a dog, there are some very basic conditions that must be considered. One of the first significant questions that must be answered is whether or not the person who will actually be given the responsibility of the dog's care actually wants a dog—particularly a giant dog like the Anatolian that demands a high level of discipline and direction. This may sound like a moot point, but wanting a dog and wanting to care for him properly do not necessarily go hand in hand.

Children are often wildly enthusiastic about having a dog and, undeniably, pets are a wonderful method of teaching children responsibility. It should be remembered, however, that childhood enthusiasm can inspire a youngster to promise anything to get what he wants, but that same enthusiasm may wane very quickly. Further, today's children have extremely busy schedules with homework, extra-curricular activities and social events. Who will take care of the puppy once the novelty wears off? Again— does that person want a dog?

When there are children in the home, it must be understood

Anatolians are born shepherds. The flock animals accept and respect these dogs and take direction from them.

that they are most likely to be considered the Anatolian's special responsibility. While he will protect them with his life if necessary, also understand that the Anatolian may not be able to distinguish a serious threat from the play-acting that your children's neighborhood friends may participate in while in your home. Your Anatolian does not want his children harmed by anyone!

It will be entirely unfair to ask your children to govern their playtime with their friends to accommodate your Anatolian. Common sense indicates that your Anatolian is put away when visiting children are present. And that does not mean in the next room with the door ajar or on the other side of some flimsy partition. If an Anatolian believes his wards are being threatened,

there are no lengths too great for him to go to rescue them.

Desire to own a dog aside, does the lifestyle of the family actually provide for responsible dog ownership? If the entire family is away from early morning to late at night, who will provide for all of a puppy's needs? Feeding, exercise time, outdoor access and the like cannot be provided if no one is at home to do it.

That the Anatolian was forced to endure the extreme climatic conditions of Turkey with no provisions for shelter made by the shepherds does not mean that the dog should be subjected to the same treatment as a pet. The breed's double coat serves to protect the Anatolian from all kinds of weather, but there should always be a place for the dog to retreat from rain and snow, and a

We're just having fun! Anatolian pups grow quickly and seem unaware of their great size...these 18-week-old pups can easily (and playfully!) overtake their owner.

shady place to rest in the heat of a summer's day.

The Anatolian requires no more than the standard care one would give any dog of its size in respect of brushing and care of the eyes, ears, foot pads and nails. The coat requires little other care except during its twice-a-year shedding periods. Vigorous daily brushing at that time will save hours of house cleaning. However, while grooming of an adult Anatolian doesn't require as much time and patience as that for the luxuriously coated breeds, that does not mean that the breed needs no grooming—on the contrary! Lacking regular brushing, an Anatolian's coat can deposit layers of loose hair on every surface in your home.

As great as claims are for an Anatolian's adaptability and intelligence, remember that there is no new dog, no matter what breed, that doesn't need to be taught every household rule that must be observed. Some dogs

catch on more quickly than others, and puppies are just as inclined to forget or disregard lessons as young human children.

The requirements for Anatolian Shepherd ownership are high. Prospective owners must be willing to give the Anatolian Shepherd all the time and patience he requires to achieve his full potential. An absolutely secure environment is needed and the need for socialization must continue on through the dog's early life. If an individual can meet the requirements of the breed, there are few breeds in the world today that can offer as much companionship and protection as Turkey's gentle guardian of the flocks.

WHY A PURE-BRED?

Many people ask why they should get a pure-bred dog in the first place if there are so many special consideration involved. Probably the major reason, outside of the

A GENTLER GIANT
The behavior and temperament of the Anatolian are usually much different out of his own domain than it is at home. Having no territory to protect, even the staunchest guardians when well socialized have proven to be excellent Therapy Dogs and have earned their Canine Good Citizenship certificates easily.

esthetic considerations, is the predictability of a pure-bred dog, a trait that is absent in mixed-breed dogs.

It is almost impossible to determine what a mixed-breed puppy will look like as an adult. More important, it is impossible to determine what the temperament of a puppy of mixed parentage is going to be like. Will he be suitable for the person or family who wishes to own him? If the puppy grows up to become too big, too hairy or too active for the owner, what then will happen to him?

Size and temperament can vary to a degree even within pure-bred dogs. Still, as stated, controlled breeding over many generations has produced dogs give us reasonable assurance of what the pure-bred puppy will look and act like when he reaches maturity. This predictability is more important than you might think.

Just about any dog whose background is made up of sound and sane individuals has the potential to become a loving companion. However, the predictability of a pure-bred dog offers reasonable insurance that the dog will suit not only the person's esthetic demands but also the owner's lifestyle.

Before you bring an Anatolian puppy into your household, visit breeders and spend as much time

TRUE TO HIS ANCESTRY
The characteristics of present-day Anatolians are not significantly different from those of the dogs that are working livestock guardians nor do those who cherish the breed want changes to occur. The breed remains protective and territorial, and adult Anatolians of the same sex may not always tolerate one another. The Anatolian needs a large area of confined space to exercise off-lead and is really not recommended or suited for life in the city.

with both puppies and adults as you can. Be sure that the adult Anatolian is the dog that appeals to you esthetically and temperamentally, and, above all, that you will be a suitable owner for the breed.

CHARACTER OF THE BREED
By this time you should be pretty well convinced of the Anatolian's ability and desire to protect. That is all well and good, but it is up to

The Anatolian is never far from his background...and never far from the flock when the opportunity arises.

you to channel the dog's desire so that this breed that has been required to make decisions on its own for thousands of years doesn't protect you and yours from that which you need no protection.

A sound Anatolian that has been well trained is entirely capable of understanding "this person is OK." Note that I said "capable of understanding." He doesn't come equipped with the ability to discern between the postman and a robber. That part is up to you.

The first Anatolian I met was "Toby," a 120-pound cream-colored male, owned by a good friend of mine. The two met me at the door and Toby looked me straight in the eye without a clue as to whether I was to be "lunch" or his new best friend. My friend just said, "OK, Toby, a friend," and then she turned to me and said, "You'll be fine to come and go now."

"Sure," I thought, "I under-stand her, but does the dog?" Evidently Toby did understand, because he and I became fast friends and I came and went over the next few days without incident.

My next encounter with the breed was a tad more intimidating in that "Jake" was on the other side of another friend's fenced property. When I drove up to the gate, I had to get out of my car to ring the bell that announced my arrival. Jake's bark and bared teeth made it clear that in no uncertain terms my side of the fence is exactly where I should remain, and remain I did until my host came down and let our protective friend know I was friend and not foe.

For the rest of my weekend there, Jake was the most amiable and fun companion I could have imagined having. He was my hiking companion and, by mutual agreement, shared the guest room with me. He would also have gladly shared my bed had there been room for both of us. It was then and there that the Anatolian earned a special place on my list of breeds that I especially admire.

SECURITY

When the Anatolian worked as a guardian of the flocks, there were no fences. Rather, he staked out the territory that his herd occupied and trespassers were not permitted within those boundaries. Most of us do not live in pastures and, if we do not, we cannot afford to allow our Anatolian to define his own perimeters. It could mean instant death to an unsuspecting stray or a neighbor's dog who did not understand that your Anatolian had included part of the road in his stakeout.

No Anatolian should be in a home that does not have a property that is secured by a fence of adequate height—*at least* 5 or 6 feet (152–183 cms)—and that has gates that can be locked. There can be no exceptions to this rule.

The Anatolian is not a dog that can be left on his own continuously. Yes, he spent little time with the shepherd in his life on the Anatolian Plateau, but don't forget, he was working then. He was not only a protector but also a member of the flock with whom he lived. Thus, he had companionship. He had something to do and lots of woolly whites to do it with. Denied the opportunity to serve and protect, the Anatolian could easily develop behavioral problems, often manifested in destructive digging.

The Anatolian is an ideal family dog in that he is able to share his devotion with every member of the family and has an innate ability to adjust his own mood to that of a particular family member. Do understand that your Anatolian will be on patrol at all times and will advise you vocally of the least suspicious sound or movement. In other words, the Anatolian barks. This is especially so with the young Anatolian who is still learning what is a threat and what isn't. Time and supervision help in this situation, but your Anatolian is going to let you know when there is anything going on that he isn't quite sure should be taking place. His only way of doing so is vocally.

TRAINING THE ANATOLIAN

Commonly used training techniques may not always work with Anatolians, and new owners should stay in touch with the breeder from whom their dog was purchased so that they can be guided through problem training periods. Force does not work with this breed, and patience is high on the list of virtues a good trainer must possess.

TRAINABILITY

When you think about training an Anatolian Shepherd, you must first stop to remember his history: as sole guardian of the flock, this dog was expected to make sound decisions based on the welfare of his charges. That takes having a mind of his own and little or no experience in blindly following orders just because someone blurted them out.

Can you train an Anatolian? The answer is yes. Will it be easy? Well, a lot will depend on the individual dog and your ability as a trainer. Don't, however, expect your Anatolian to do things like dash off after and retrieve a ball 88 times in a row. The Anatolian is more apt to assume if you've thrown something away, you probably don't want it. And if he does bring the ball or tossed item back to you and you immediately throw it again, he's far more apt to give you a puzzled look that tells you he thinks you've taken leave of your senses. In other words, blind and seemingly pointless obedience is not the Anatolian's strong suit. Anatolians have acquired obedience degrees in competitions, but I wouldn't anticipate their pressing Goldens or Border Collies in accumulating top awards.

There are times when your Anatolian needs correction, and you must be forthright and uncompromising in this respect. This, however, never means striking your dog. A rap on the nose with a finger or holding his head in your hands with eye-to-eye contact and a stern "No!" may well be necessary. The young alpha-type Anatolian male partic-ularly can try and flex his dominance muscles. He must be made to understand that it is you who establishes and maintains law and order. Firmness will not shatter the Anatolian, but harsh methods can destroy the dog's personality and trainability.

Repetition and determination work best with the breed and, once learned, lessons seem almost a natural part of the Anatolian's character. Avoidance of bad habits works best. Not allowing unwanted behavior to occur in the first place is infinitely simpler than trying to convince your Anatolian to stop something he has been doing all along.

WITH OTHER PETS AND ANIMALS
Our Anatolian friend Toby lives in a home that also includes what I refer to as an entire "flock" of Papillons. When visiting there, I have watched in awe as the Papillons—adults and puppies—climb over and under this quadruple-dip vanilla mountain. The oldsters cuddle up next to him to keep warm and the puppies dangle happily off his ears. When the "Papillon Wrecking Crew" gets to be too much for the patience of this gentle giant, he simply nudges them aside and then stands by patiently for the next assault. But let a stranger or strange dog even threaten to harm a member of his little flock and Toby is ready, willing and able to turn himself into a canine tornado capable of taking down a full-grown man.

This is the same dog that amazingly plays sentry the minute he realizes one of the Papillon mothers-to-be is about to commence whelping. And this he knows long before there are any signs discernible to the humans who are in residence. No man or beast is permitted beyond the whelping room door other than his owner or the individuals to which his owner gives the OK, and then only when she is present.

Another Anatolian whom I got to know on a one-to-one basis is owned by a young lady who suffers from a physical disability. She uses her friend and companion as an assistance dog. He is always directly at her side to steady and support the woman to whom he is so obviously devoted.

Her Anatolian accompanies her everywhere, but I see them most often at dog shows where strange dogs of all shapes and sizes pass by. Her boy, however, ignores them all and usually will be seen fast asleep in the corner of a room somewhere just far enough away where he can keep a closed but somehow still watchful eye on his mistress. All his owner needs to do is attempt to rise from her chair and he is at her side. His awareness and keen sensitivity to her needs are remarkable and touching.

Your Anatolian would be no less diligent, watchful and tolerant if your other pets were cats, rodents or birds. But do note that I said *your* other pets. Woe be to the strange dog or other beast

that might trespass! It had better be fleet of foot!

HEALTH CONCERNS IN THE ANATOLIAN BREED

The Anatolian Shepherd is still close to his Spartan working dog origins and presently has few significant genetic problems to

DOGS, DOGS, GOOD FOR YOUR HEART!
People usually purchase dogs for companionship, but studies show that dogs can help to improve their owners' health and level of activity, as well as lower a human's risk of coronary heart disease. Without even realizing it, when a person puts time into exercising, grooming and feeding a dog, he also puts more time into his own personal health care. Dog owners establish more routine schedules for their dogs to follow, which can have positive effects on their own health. Dogs also teach us patience, offer unconditional love and provide the joy of having a furry friend to pet!

concern new owners or breeders. The breed lives to a surprisingly old age for a dog so large. A well-cared-for Anatolian may easily live to be 11 or 12, many into their teens. Like all large dogs, however, the breed can occasionally be susceptible to hip and elbow problems, but responsible breeders continue to have their dogs x-rayed and seek certification for all breeding stock. The Anatolian can be extremely sensitive to anesthesia and anyone owning the breed should advise his vet of this problem. It is important to remind vets and their technicians of this periodically to avoid its being overlooked in notes kept on your dog.

Another congenital defect occasionally found in the breed is entropion, a condition in which the eyelid rolls in toward the eye, allowing the lashes to rub against and irritate the cornea. It is important to consult your vet if excessive tearing or irritation persists.

Some instances of hypothyroidism have been reported in the breed as well. Hypothyroidism is a condition in which the thyroid gland malfunctions, resulting in reduced output. The signs may include poor coat, lethargy and weakness, along with poor appetite in spite of increased weight gain. Treatment usually requires long-term, even lifetime, medication.

Although bloat (gastric torsion or dilatation) is not actually known to be an inherited problem, it does occur often in large deep-chested breeds such as the Anatolian. Little is known about the actual cause of bloat. Many theories have been offered, but none actually proven. This often-fatal condition seems to occur frequently at night after the dog has had a large meal, ingested a great deal of water and then exercises strenuously.

Symptoms can range from a severe attack of gas to death. It can occur so suddenly and swiftly that only *immediate* attention by a vet experienced in dealing with the condition will save your dog's life.

Simply described, bloat causes the stomach to rotate so that both ends are closed off. The food contained in the stomach ferments but the gases cannot escape, thereby causing the stomach to swell, greatly pressuring the entire diaphragm and consequently leading to extreme cardiac and respiratory complications. The affected dog is in extreme pain and death can follow very quickly unless the gas is released through surgery. Again, immediate veterinary assistance is necessary if your dog displays any symptoms of bloat. Symptoms and prevention are discussed at more length in the health chapter.

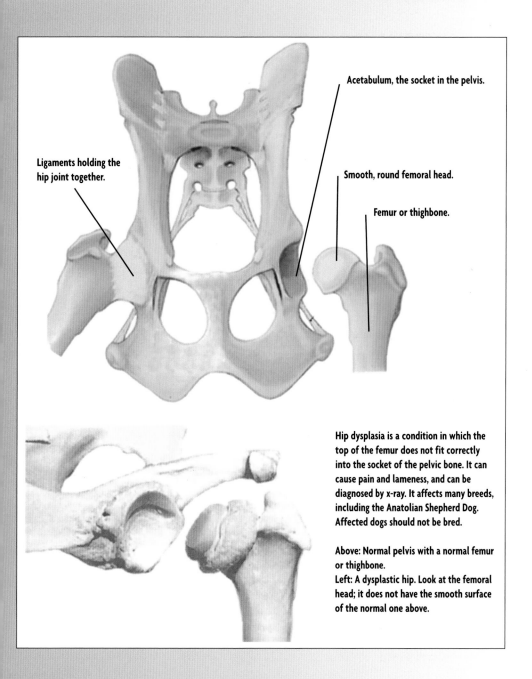

Acetabulum, the socket in the pelvis.

Ligaments holding the hip joint together.

Smooth, round femoral head.

Femur or thighbone.

Hip dysplasia is a condition in which the top of the femur does not fit correctly into the socket of the pelvic bone. It can cause pain and lameness, and can be diagnosed by x-ray. It affects many breeds, including the Anatolian Shepherd Dog. Affected dogs should not be bred.

Above: Normal pelvis with a normal femur or thighbone.
Left: A dysplastic hip. Look at the femoral head; it does not have the smooth surface of the normal one above.

BREED STANDARD FOR THE
ANATOLIAN SHEPHERD DOG

INTRODUCTION TO THE STANDARD

In the earliest days of man's relationship with dogs, he began to see that those dogs constructed in a certain way were more successful at performing the tasks assigned to them. It then became those particular characteristics that guided man's breeding practices. The people who kept the dogs that were serving them best gathered to make comparisons and seek out stock to improve their own dogs. The more successful keepers were asked to observe the dogs at work and evaluate them.

With industrialization, little villages grew into large cities and towns and the citizenry moved into urban dwellings. Fewer dogs were given the opportunity to perform in the capacity for which their breeds were created. To avoid the respective breeds' losing their ability to perform, dog fanciers began to select their stock on the basis of the conformation that they determined would produce the most successful workers. The guidelines became theoretical rather than practical.

In the case of the Anatolian Shepherd Dog, as far back in time as one wishes to trace, the same characteristics were important. The dog had to be large enough and strong enough to handle predators of all sizes and degrees of aggressiveness. He had to be protective and of a calm demeanor to coexist with the flocks he attended. These characteristics typify the breed and remain paramount in the minds of breeders who champion the cause of the Anatolian today.

It should be noted here that these descriptions, written by knowledgeable individuals in the breed for their peers, were the forerunners of what are known today as breed standards. The descriptions were used primarily as checklists or blueprints to breed by and they served as reminders so that important points of conformation would not be lost.

Today's Anatolian Shepherd Dog breed standard describes a dog that is entirely capable of performing the duties it has been called upon to perform for thousands of years. It includes a description of ideal structure,

Outward appearance means nothing without correct structure underneath. Show judges use a hands-on approach to evaluating the dog's physical conformation.

temperament, coat, color and the manner in which the breed moves (gait). All of these descriptions relate directly to the breed's original purpose.

As stated, breed standards are used by breeders to assist them in breeding toward this goal of perfection. While no dog is absolutely perfect, the dogs that adhere most closely to the ideal are what breeders will determine are show or breeding stock. The standard is also used by dog show judges to compare actual dogs to the ideal. The dog adhering most closely to this ideal, in the judge's opinion, is then the winner of his class and so on down the line.

THE AMERICAN KENNEL CLUB STANDARD FOR THE ANATOLIAN SHEPHERD DOG

GENERAL APPEARANCE

Large, rugged, powerful and impressive, possessing great endurance and agility. Developed through a set of very demanding circumstances for a purely utilitarian purpose; he is a working guard dog without equal, with a unique ability to protect livestock. General impression—Appears bold, but calm, unless challenged. He possesses size, good bone, a well-muscled torso with a strong head. Reserve out of his territory is acceptable.

An Anatolian dog of correct type, balance and substance.

Fluid movement and even temperament is desirable.

SIZE, PROPORTION, SUBSTANCE
General balance is more important than absolute size. Dogs should be from 29 inches and weighing from 110 to 150 pounds proportionate to size and structure. Bitches should be from 27 inches, weighing from 80 to 120 pounds, proportionate to size and structure. Neither dog nor bitch appear fat. Both dog and bitch should be rectangular, in direct proportion to height. Measurements and weights apply at age 2 or older.

HEAD
Expression should be intelligent. Eyes are medium size, set apart, almond shaped and dark brown to light amber in color. Blue eyes or eyes of two different colors are a disqualification. Eye rims will be black or brown and without sag or looseness of haw. Incomplete pigment is a serious fault. Ears should be set on no higher than the plane of the head. V-shaped, rounded apex, measuring about 4 inches at the base to 6 inches in length. The tip should be just long enough to reach the outside corner of the eyelid. Ears dropped to sides. Erect ears are a disqualification. Skull is large but in proportion to the body. There is a slight center-line furrow, fore and aft, from

Head study, showing pleasing type and structure.

apparent stop to moderate occiput. Broader in dogs than in bitches. Muzzle is blockier and stronger for the dog, but neither dog nor bitch would have a snipey head or muzzle. Nose and flews must be solid black or brown. Seasonal fading is not to be penalized. Incomplete pigment is a serious fault. Flews are normally dry but pronounced enough to contribute to "squaring" the overall muzzle appearance. Teeth and gums strong and healthy. Scissors bite preferred, level bite acceptable. Broken teeth are not to be faulted. Overshot, undershot or wry bite are disqualifications.

NECK, TOPLINE, BODY
Neck slightly arched, powerful, and muscular, moderate in length with more skin and fur than

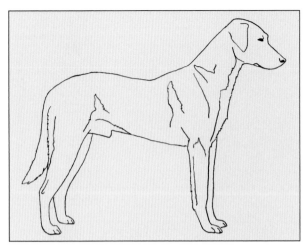

Above:
Faults: General lack of power, bone and substance; weak topline; flat feet; weak pasterns.
Below:
Faults: Too coarse and Mastiff-like; upright shoulders; lack of angulation in rear.

Never fat or soft. Chest is deep (to the elbow) and well-sprung with a distinct tuck up at the loin. Tail should be long and reaching to the hocks. Set on rather high. When relaxed, it is carried low with the end curled upwards. When alert, the tail is carried high, making a "wheel." Both low and wheel carriage are acceptable, when gaiting. Wheel carriage preferred. The tail will not necessarily uncurl totally.

FOREQUARTERS

Shoulders should be muscular and well developed, blades long, broad and sloping. Elbows should be neither in nor out. Forelegs should be relatively long, well-boned and set straight with strong pasterns. The feet are strong and compact with well-arched toes, oval in shape. They should have stout nails with pads thick and tough. Dewclaws may be removed.

elsewhere on the body, forming a protective ruff. The dewlap should not be pendulous and excessive. Topline will appear level when gaiting. Back will be powerful, muscular, and level, with drop behind withers and gradual arch over loin, sloping slightly downward at the croup. Body well proportioned, functional, without exaggeration.

HINDQUARTERS

Strong, with broad thighs and heavily muscled. Angulation at the stifle and hock is in proportion to the forequarters. As seen from behind, the legs are parallel. The feet are strong and compact with well-arched toes, oval in shape. Double dewclaws may exist. Dewclaws may be removed.

COAT

Short (1 inch minimum, not tight) to Rough (approximately 4

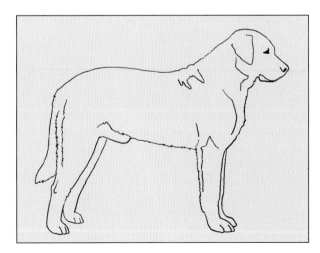

inches in length) with neck hair slightly longer. Somewhat longer and thicker at the neck and mane. A thick undercoat is common to all. Feathering may occur on the ear fringes, legs, breeching, and tail.

COLOR
All color patterns and markings are equally acceptable.

GAIT
At the trot, the gait is powerful yet fluid. When viewed from the front or rear, the legs turn neither in nor out, nor do feet cross or interfere with each other. With increased speed, footfall converges toward the center line of gravity. When viewed from the side, the front legs should reach out smoothly with no obvious pounding. The withers and backline should stay nearly level with little rise or fall. The rear assembly should push out smoothly with hocks doing their share of the work and flexing well.

TEMPERAMENT
Alert and intelligent, calm and observant. Instinctively protective, he is courageous and highly adaptable. He is very loyal and responsive. Highly territorial, he is a natural guard. Reserve around strangers and off his territory is acceptable. Responsiveness with animation is not

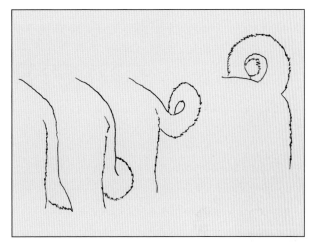

characteristic of the breed. Overhandling would be discouraged.

DISQUALIFICATIONS
Blue eyes or eyes of two different colors. Erect ears. Overshot, undershot, or wry bite.

Approved: June 1995
Effective: June 1, 1996

Above: Tail carriage in the Anatolian can be an indication of mood and attention level, ranging from relaxed (left) to highly alert (right), and stages in between. Below: Faults: Dip behind shoulders; high in rear; lack of rear angulation.

ANATOLIAN SHEPHERD DOG

SELECTING AN ANATOLIAN BREEDER AND PUPPY

Your Anatolian should only be purchased from a breeder who has earned a reputation for consistently producing dogs that are mentally and physically sound. The only way a breeder can earn this reputation is through selective breeding aimed at eliminating genetic weaknesses.

The first question a prospective owner should ask an Anatolian breeder is, "What do you do with your dogs?" If the person to whom you are talking breeds Anatolians only to sell—go somewhere else for your dog! Dedicated Anatolian breeders belong to their breed club, compete at shows and are adamant about proper socialization of their dogs.

These same people are very much aware of who else in the breed does or does not ascribe to the parent club's rigid Code of Ethics. It is a requirement of the club that all dogs are hip scored to ascertain the degree, if any, of hip problems. In fact, breeders who maintain membership in the parent club monitor their litters carefully in order to avoid defects of any kind. These are the individuals that you can depend upon to obtain a sound, well-bred and well-socialized representative of the Anatolian Shepherd Dog breed.

The first clue that tells you how much the breeder cares about his dogs is the cleanliness of the area in which the dogs are kept. The next is how well socialized the parents of the litter are. Those two conditions met, you can proceed to look at the puppies themselves.

The Anatolian puppy you buy should be a happy and bouncy extrovert. However, you need not necessarily select the leader of the little pack. The extremely big, bold and extroverted pup may prove to be a bit more than the inexperienced Anatolian owner is equipped to handle. This does not mean you should select a shy, shrinking-violet puppy; this is not typical of correct Anatolian attitude at all.

The breeder may ask you so many questions that you may feel you are on trial in the courts. In a way, you are! The breeder is weighing whether or not you would make a good owner of his Anatolian pup and, if so, which puppy in the litter would be most suitable for you.

Healthy Anatolian puppies are strong and firm to the touch, never bony or, on the other hand, obese and bloated. Coats will be lustrous with no sign of dry or flaky skin. The inside of the puppy's ears should be pink and clean. Dark discharge or a bad odor could indicate ear mites, a sure sign of poor maintenance.

The healthy Anatolian puppy's breath smells sweet. The teeth are clean and white, and there should never be any malfor-mation of the mouth or jaw. The puppy's eyes should be clear and bright. Eyes that appear runny and irritated indicate serious problems. There should be no sign of discharge from the nose nor should it ever be crusted or runny. Coughing and diarrhea are danger signals, as are any eruptions on the skin.

The healthy and sound Anatolian puppy's front legs should be straight as little posts. Even at an early age, an Anatolian puppy's legs appear long in proportion and may give the youngster somewhat of an awkward gangly look. Still, movement is true and there should be no hint of lameness or other difficulty in moving about.

The question of male or female arises invariably when selecting a puppy. The Anatolian Shepherd Dog is a large breed to

Male or female? Pet or show? What color? These are just some of the decisions you should make before visiting the litter, when you'll likely be overwhelmed by the furry babies and unable to think straight!

It's hard to imagine the large, strong dog that the baby Anatolian will grow to be.

begin with, and males are the larger of the two sexes, often measuring anywhere from 3–6 inches (7–14 cms) taller at the shoulder and weighing as much as 30–50 pounds (about 13.5–23 kgs) over what the average female might weigh. Males are also inclined to be more aggressive than their sisters.

These are important considerations because not everyone is physically capable of keeping a 150-pound (69-kg) dog under control. Any dog, no matter how well trained, can become very excited and forget manners for a minute or two. Those two minutes could send a less able person tumbling end over end.

Females are inclined to be especially good with children and a little more lady-like in the home. The problem that can arise, however, is that some females become overzealous in protecting their little people and in keeping intruders off their property.

It should be understood that none of the considerations outlined is carved in stone. Not all males are extremely large nor are all of them unduly aggressive. Some females can grow to be well above average in size and they do have their semi-annual heat cycles sometime after they have passed a year of age. A watchful eye is necessary at this time to avoid unwanted puppies being sired by some marauding male. Spaying the female and neutering the male saves the pet owner the headaches of most all of the sexually related problems without significantly changing the character of the breed.

If the prospective owner is considering a show career for his puppy, he should be aware that the most any breeder can offer is an opinion on the "show

A HEALTHY PUP

You should not even think about buying a puppy that looks sick, undernourished, overly frightened or nervous. Sometimes a timid puppy will warm up to you after a 30-minute "let's-get-acquainted" session.

potential" of a young puppy. Any predictions breeders make about a puppy's future are based upon their experience with past litters that have produced winning show dogs. It is obvious that the more successful a breeder has been in producing winning Anatolians over the years, the broader his base of comparison will be. Give serious consideration to both what the standard says a show-quality Anatolian must look like and to the breeder's recommendations.

PREPARING PUPPY'S PLACE IN YOUR HOME

Researching your breed and finding a breeder are only two aspects of the homework you will have to do before collecting your Anatolian puppy. You will also have to prepare your home and family for the new addition. Much as you would prepare a nursery for a newborn baby, you will need to designate a place in your home that will be the puppy's own. How you prepare your home will depend on how much freedom the dog will be allowed. Whatever you decide, you must ensure that he has a place that he can "call his own."

When you bring your new puppy into your home, you are bringing him into what will become his home as well. Obviously, you did not buy a puppy with the intentions of catering to his every whim and

allowing him to "rule the roost," but in order for a puppy to grow into a stable, well-adjusted dog, he has to feel comfortable in his surroundings. Remember, he is leaving the warmth and security of his mother and littermates, as well as the familiarity of the only place he has ever known, so it is important to make his transition as easy as possible. By preparing a

TEMPERAMENT COUNTS

Your selection of a good puppy can be determined by your needs. A show potential or a good pet? It is your choice. Every puppy, however, should be of good temperament. Although show-quality puppies are bred and raised with emphasis on physical conformation, responsible breeders strive for equally good temperament. Do not buy from a breeder who concentrates solely on physical beauty at the expense of personality.

Training from puppyhood is essential if you are to control such a powerful dog as an adult. Basic training includes acclimating the pup to his lead and everyday collar.

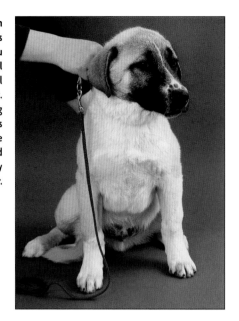

YOUR SCHEDULE . . .
If you lead an erratic, unpredictable life, with daily or weekly changes in your work requirements, consider the problems of owning a puppy. The new puppy has to be fed regularly, socialized (loved, petted, handled, introduced to other people) and, most importantly, allowed to go outdoors for house-training. As the dog gets older, he can be more tolerant of deviations in his feeding and relief schedule.

place in your home for the puppy, you are making him feel as welcome as possible in a strange new place. It should not take him long to get used to it, but the sudden shock of being transplanted is somewhat traumatic for a young pup. Imagine how a small child would feel in the same situation—that is how your puppy must be feeling. It is up to you to comfort and reassure him.

WHAT YOU SHOULD BUY

CRATE

To someone unfamiliar with the use of crates in dog training, it may seem like punishment to shut a dog in a crate, but this is not the case at all. Although all breeders do not advocate crate training for large-breed dogs, many breeders and trainers are recommending crates as preferred tools for pet puppies as well as show puppies.

Crates have many humane and highly effective uses in dog care and training. For example, crate

PUPPY APPEARANCE
Your puppy should have a well-fed appearance but not a distended abdomen, which may indicate worms or incorrect feeding, or both. The body should be firm, with a solid feel. The skin of the abdomen should be pale pink and clean, without signs of scratching or rash. Check the legs to see if the dewclaws have been removed. Double dewclaws may be present on the hindlegs.

PET INSURANCE

Just like you can insure your car, your house and your own health, you likewise can insure your dog's health. Investigate a pet insurance policy by talking to your vet. Depending on the age of your dog, the breed and the kind of coverage you desire, your policy can be very affordable. Most policies cover accidental injuries, poisoning and thousands of medical problems and illnesses, including cancers. Some carriers also offer routine care and immunization coverage, including heartworm preventative, prescription flea control, annual checkups, teeth cleaning, spaying/neutering, health screening and more. These policies are more costly than the others, but may be well worth the investment.

training is a popular and successful house-training method. In addition, a crate can keep your dog safe during travel and, perhaps most importantly, a crate provides your dog with a place of his own in your home. It serves as a "doggie bedroom" of sorts—your Anatolian puppy can curl up in his crate when he wants to sleep or when he just needs a break. The Anatolian should not be left in his crate for extended periods of more than a few hours. Since an Anatolian cannot guard your home from his crate, your puppy needn't spend the night in his crate. With soft bedding and his favorite toy, a crate becomes a cozy pseudo-den for your dog. Like his ancestors, he too will seek out the comfort and retreat of a den—you just happen to be providing him with something a little more luxurious than what his early ancestors enjoyed.

As far as purchasing a crate, the type that you buy is up to you. It will most likely be one of the two most popular types: wire or fiberglass. There are advantages and disadvantages to each type. The wire crate is more open,

QUALITY FOOD

The cost of food must be mentioned. All dogs need a good-quality food with the correct amount of protein to develop their bones and muscles properly. Most dogs are not picky eaters but, unless fed properly, can quickly succumb to skin problems.

PHOTO COURTESY OF DOSKOCIL

fine for an eight-week-old Anatolian pup, but it will not do him much good for long! A giant-size crate, at least 32 inches (81 cms) wide x 48 inches (123 cms) deep x 35 inches (89 cms) high will be necessary for a full-grown Anatolian.

BEDDING

A soft crate pad will help the dog feel more at home in his crate, and you may also like to provide a small blanket. First, this will take the place of the leaves, twigs, etc., that the pup would use in the

allowing the air to flow through and affording the dog a view of what is going on around him. A fiberglass crate is sturdier and can double as an air-travel crate, making it preferred by most Anatolian keepers. The size of the crate is another thing to consider. Puppies do not stay puppies forever—in fact, sometimes it seems as if they grow right before your eyes. A small crate may be

CRATE-TRAINING TIPS

During crate training, you should partition off the section of the crate in which the pup stays. If he is given too big an area, this will hinder your training efforts. Crate training is based on the fact that a dog does not like to soil his sleeping quarters, so it is ineffective to keep a pup in an area that is so big that he can eliminate in one end and get far enough away from it to sleep. Also, you want to make the crate den-like for the pup. Blankets and a favorite toy will make the crate cozy for the small pup; as he grows, you may want to evict some of his "roommates" to make more room. It will take some coaxing at first, but be patient. Given some time to get used to it, your pup will adapt to his new home-within-a-home quite nicely.

Your Anatolian's crate will be large enough to hold an entire litter, as the crate you purchase for your puppy should be of a suitable size to accommodate the full-grown adult.

wild to make a den; the pup can make his own "burrow" in the crate. Although your pup is far removed from his den-making ancestors, the denning instinct is still a part of his genetic makeup. Second, until you take your pup home, he has been sleeping amid the warmth of his mother and littermates, and while a blanket is not the same as a warm, breathing body, it still provides heat and something with which to snuggle. You will want to wash your pup's bedding frequently in case he has a house-training mishap in his crate, and replace or remove any blanket that becomes ragged and starts to fall apart.

Toys
Toys are a must for dogs of all ages, especially for curious playful pups. Puppies are the "children" of the dog world, and

what child does not love toys? Chew toys provide enjoyment for both dog and owner—your dog will enjoy playing with his favorite toys, while you will enjoy the fact that they distract him from chewing on your expensive shoes and leather sofa. Puppies love to chew; in fact, chewing is a physical need for pups as they are teething, and everything looks appetizing! The full range of your possessions—from cotton slipper to Oriental carpet—are fair game in the eyes of a teething pup. Puppies are not all that discerning when it comes to finding something literally to "sink their teeth into"—everything tastes great!

Though not inveterate chewers, a bored Anatolian with nothing to do and insufficient human contact can become a destructive Anatolian. Chewing is one way the breed can release some of the frustration that builds up. To avoid that occurring, select toys for both puppies and adults that are designed for large, powerfully jawed dogs and make sure your dog is receiving the attention he deserves.

Squeaky toys are quite popular, but must be avoided for the Anatolian. Perhaps a squeaky toy can be used as an aid in training, but not for free play. If a pup "disembowels" one of these, the small plastic squeaker inside

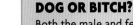

DOG OR BITCH?
Both the male and female Anatolian make excellent companions and are equally alert and protective. Their primary difference is in height and weight, and sometimes in abundance of coat, with males being greater in these respects. Young males can become especially assertive as they approach sexual maturity and require a firm hand so that bad habits are not established.

can be dangerous if swallowed. Monitor the condition of all your pup's toys carefully and get rid of any that have been chewed to the point of becoming potentially dangerous.

Be careful of natural bones, which have a tendency to splinter into sharp, dangerous pieces. Also be careful of rawhide, which can turn into pieces that are easy to swallow and become a mushy mess on your carpet.

LEASH

A nylon leash is probably the best option, as it is the most resistant to puppy teeth should your pup take a liking to chewing on his leash. Of course, this is a habit that should be nipped in the bud, but, if your pup likes to chew on his leash, he has a very slim chance of being able to chew through the strong nylon. Nylon leashes are also lightweight, which is good for a young Anatolian who is just getting used to the idea of walking on a leash. For everyday walking and safety purposes, the nylon leash is a good choice.

Of course, there are leads designed for training purposes and specially made harnesses, but these are likely not necessary for routine walks.

TOYS, TOYS, TOYS!

With a big variety of dog toys available, and so many that look like they would be a lot of fun for a dog, be careful in your selection. It is amazing what a set of puppy teeth can do to an innocent-looking toy; so, obviously, safety is a major consideration. Be sure to choose the most durable products that you can find. Hard nylon bones and toys are a safe bet, and many of them are offered in different scents and flavors that will be sure to capture your dog's attention. It is always fun to play a game of fetch with your dog, and there are balls and flying discs that are specially made to withstand dog teeth.

There are many types of leashes available. For a puppy, a light nylon leash will suffice, while the adult will require a thicker, stronger leash.

COLLAR

Your pup should get used to wearing a collar all the time since you will want to attach his identification tags to it; plus, you have to attach the leash to something! A lightweight nylon collar is a good choice. Make certain that the collar fits snugly enough so that the pup cannot wriggle out of it, but is loose enough so that it will not be uncomfortably tight around the pup's neck. You should be able to fit a finger between the pup's neck and the collar. It may take some time for your pup to get used to wearing the collar, but soon he will not even notice it. A sturdy leather collar will be necessary for the adolescent and adult Anatolian. Choke collars are made for training, but should only

be used by those who know *exactly* how to use it.

FOOD AND WATER BOWLS

Your pup will need two bowls, one for food and one for water. You may want two sets of bowls, one for indoors and one for

A spiked collar as used on the Anatolian Shepherd Dog in his homeland. It is worn with the spikes facing outward to protect the dog's neck from attacks by bears, wolves, other dogs, etc.

CHOOSE AN APPROPRIATE COLLAR

The **BUCKLE COLLAR** is the standard collar used for everyday purposes. Be sure that you adjust the buckle on growing puppies. Check it every day. It can become too tight overnight! These collars can be made of leather or nylon. Attach your dog's identification tags to this collar.

The **CHOKE COLLAR** is constructed of highly polished steel so that it slides easily through the stainless steel loop. The idea is that the dog controls the pressure around his neck and he will stop pulling if the collar becomes uncomfortable. It is used *only* for training and should *never* be left on a dog.

The **HALTER** is for a trained dog that has to be restrained to prevent running away, chasing a cat and the like. Considered the most humane of all collars, it is frequently used on smaller dogs on which collars are not comfortable.

Your local pet shop will have an array of dishes and bowls suitable for the food and water you offer your Anatolian Shepherd Dog.

Photo courtesy of Mikki Pet Products.

outdoors. Purchase the largest size you can find. Stainless steel or sturdy plastic bowls are popular. Plastic bowls are more chewable, but dogs tend not to chew on the steel variety, which can be sterilized. It is important to buy sturdy bowls since anything is in danger of being chewed by puppy teeth and you do not want your dog to constantly chew apart his bowl (for his safety and for your financial stability!). Bowl stands on which to elevate the bowls should be considered a requirement, as this prevents bloat.

CLEANING SUPPLIES

Until a pup is house-trained you will be doing a lot of cleaning. "Accidents" will occur, which is acceptable in the beginning stages of house-training because the puppy does not know any better. All you can do is be prepared to clean up any accidents as soon as they happen. Old rags, towels, newspapers and a safe disinfectant are good to have on hand.

BEYOND THE BASICS

The items previously discussed are the bare necessities. You will find out what else you need as you go along—grooming supplies, flea/tick protection, baby gates to partition a room, etc. These things will vary depending on your situation, but it is important that you have everything you need to feed and make your Anatolian comfortable in his first few days at home.

PUPPY-PROOFING YOUR HOME
Aside from making sure that your Anatolian will be comfortable in your home, you also have to make sure that your home is safe for your Anatolian. This means taking precautions that your pup will not get into anything he should not get into and that there is nothing within his reach that may harm him should he sniff it, chew it, inspect it, etc. This probably seems obvious since, while you are primarily concerned with your pup's safety, at the same time you do not want your belongings to be ruined. Breakables should be placed out of reach if your dog is to have full run of the house. If he is to be limited to certain places within the house, keep any potentially dangerous items in the "off-limits" areas.

An electrical cord can pose a danger should the puppy decide to taste it—and who is going to convince a pup that it would not make a great chew toy? Cords should be fastened tightly against the wall. If your dog is going to spend time in a crate, make sure that there is nothing near his crate that he can reach if he sticks his curious little nose or paws through the openings. Just as you would with a child, keep all household cleaners and chemicals where the pup cannot reach them.

It is your responsibility to clean up after your dog has relieved himself. Pet shops have various aids to assist in the cleanup job.

It is also important to make sure that the outside of your home is safe. Of course, your puppy should never be unsupervised, but a pup let loose on your fenced property will want to run and explore, and he should be granted that freedom. Do not let a fence give you a false sense of security. With nothing else to do, the neglected Anatolian can dig a hole that appears to reach to the center of the Earth! Also, the average-height fence will not deter the Anatolian if he feels there is good need for his being on the other side. A proper fence should be no less than 5–6 feet (152–183 cms). Be sure to repair or secure any gaps in the fence. Check the fence periodically to ensure that it

At 18 weeks of age, this Anatolian is growing fast and will continue to mature and fill out for many months to come.

an appointment arranged for your pup before you pick him up.

The pup's first visit will consist of an overall examination to make sure that the pup does not have any problems that are not apparent to you. The vet will also set up a schedule for the pup's vaccinations; the breeder will inform you of which ones the pup has already received and the vet can continue from there.

INTRODUCTION TO THE FAMILY

Everyone in the house will be excited about the puppy's coming home and will want to pet him and play with him, but it is best to make the introduction low-key so as not to overwhelm the puppy.

is in good shape and make repairs as needed; a very determined pup may return to the same spot to "work on it" until he is able to get through.

FIRST TRIP TO THE VET

You have selected your puppy, and your home and family are ready. Now all you have to do is collect your Anatolian from the breeder and the fun begins, right? Well...not so fast. Something else you need to plan is your pup's first trip to the vet. Perhaps the breeder can recommend someone in the area who knows large-breed dogs, a most important criterion in selecting a vet for your Anatolian, or maybe you know some other owners who can suggest a good vet. Either way, you should have

REACHING MATURITY

It is important that a prospective buyer see as many full-grown Anatolians as possible in that the breed is much larger than many people are aware. Puppies can reach 35 pounds (16 kgs) by the time they are 8 weeks old and well over 100 pounds (46 kgs) at maturity. On the other hand, for their great size, the breed is a very slow one to mature—some lines taking almost four full years before complete maturity is reached. The growing Anatolian is capable of consuming large quantities of food, but the food requirements drop sharply once maturity is achieved.

He is apprehensive already. It is the first time he has been separated from his mother and the breeder, and the ride to your home is likely to be the first time he has been in a car. The last thing you want to do is smother him, as this will only frighten him further. This is not to say that human contact is not extremely necessary at this stage, because this is the time when a connection between the pup and his human family is formed. Gentle petting and soothing words should help console him, as well as just putting him down and letting him explore on his own (under your watchful eye, of course).

The pup may approach the family members or may busy himself with exploring for a while. Gradually, each person should spend some time with the pup, one at a time, crouching down to get as close to the pup's level as possible, letting him sniff their hands and petting him gently. He definitely needs human attention and he needs to be touched—this is how to form an immediate bond. Just remember

NATURAL TOXINS
Examine your lawn and home landscaping before bringing your puppy home. Many varieties of plants have leaves, stems or flowers that are toxic if ingested, and you can depend on a curious puppy to investigate them. Ask your vet for information on poisonous plants or research them at your library.

that the pup is experiencing many things for the first time, at the same time. There are new people, new noises, new smells and new things to investigate, so be gentle, be affectionate and be as comforting as you can be.

PUP'S FIRST NIGHT HOME
You have traveled home with your new charge safely in his crate. He's been to the vet for a thorough

TOXIC PLANTS
Many plants can be toxic to dogs. If you see your dog carrying a piece of vegetation in his mouth, approach him in a quiet, disinterested manner, avoid eye contact, pet him and gradually remove the plant from his mouth. Alternatively, offer him a treat and maybe he'll drop the plant on his own accord. Be sure no toxic plants are growing in your own yard.

checkup; he's been weighed, his papers have been examined and perhaps he's even been vaccinated and wormed as well. He's met (and licked!) the whole family, including the excited children and the less-than-happy cat. He's explored his area, his new bed, the yard and anywhere else he's been permitted. He's eaten his first meal at home and relieved himself in the proper place. He's heard lots of new sounds, smelled new friends and seen more of the outside world than ever before…and that was just the first day! He's worn out and is ready for bed…or so you think!

It's puppy's first night home and you are ready to say "Good night." Keep in mind that this is his first night ever to be sleeping alone. His dam and littermates are no longer at paw's length and he's a bit scared, cold and lonely. Be reassuring to your new family member, but this is not the time to spoil him and give in to his inevitable whining.

Puppies whine. They whine to let others know where they are and hopefully to get company out of it. Place your pup in his new bed or crate in his designated area. Mercifully, he may fall asleep without a peep. When the inevitable occurs, however, ignore the whining—he is fine. Be strong and keep his best interest in mind. Do not allow yourself to feel guilty and visit the pup. He will fall asleep eventually.

Many breeders recommend placing a piece of bedding from the pup's former home in his new bed so that he recognizes and is comforted by the scent of his littermates. Others still advise placing a hot water bottle in the bed for warmth. The latter may be a good idea provided the pup doesn't attempt to suckle—he'll get good and wet, and may not fall asleep so fast.

Puppy's first night can be somewhat stressful for both the pup and his new family. Remember that you are setting the tone of nighttime at your house. Unless you want to play with your pup every night at 10 p.m., midnight and 2 a.m., don't initiate the habit. Your family will thank you, and so will your pup!

PREVENTING PUPPY PROBLEMS

SOCIALIZATION

Now that you have done all of the preparatory work and have helped your pup get accustomed to his new home and family, it is about time for you to have some fun! Socializing your Anatolian pup gives you the opportunity to show off your new friend—likely you will be the first person on your block with such an intriguing rare breed—and your pup gets to reap the benefits of being an adorable furry creature that people will want to pet and, in general, think is absolutely precious!

A puppy's investigations can lead to an upset stomach. A thirsty pup may be tempted by a carton of milk, but he will likely regret his decision later.

Besides getting to know his new family, your puppy should be exposed to other people, animals and situations. This will help him become well adjusted as he grows up and less prone to being timid or fearful of the new things he will encounter. Of course, he must not come into close contact with dogs you don't know well until his course of injections is fully complete.

Your pup's socialization began with the breeder, but now it is your responsibility to continue it. The socialization he receives until the age of 12 weeks is the most critical, as this is the time when he forms his impressions of the outside world. Be especially careful during the eight-to-ten-week-old period, also known as the fear period. The interaction he receives during this time should be gentle and reassuring. Lack of socialization, and/or negative experiences during the socialization period, can manifest itself in fear and aggression as the dog grows up. Your puppy needs lots of positive interaction, which of course includes human contact, affection, handling and exposure to other animals.

Once your pup has received his necessary vaccinations, feel free to take him out and about (on his leash, of course). Walk him around the neighborhood, take him on your daily errands, let people pet him, let him meet other dogs and pets, etc. Puppies do not have to try to make friends; there will be no shortage of people who will want to introduce themselves. Just make sure that you carefully supervise each meeting. If the neighborhood children want to say hello, for example, that is great—children and pups most often make great companions. However, sometimes an excited child can unintention-

ally handle a pup too roughly, or an overzealous pup can playfully nip a little too hard. You want to make socialization experiences positive ones. What a pup learns during this very formative stage will affect his attitude toward future encounters. You want your dog to be comfortable around everyone. A pup that has a bad experience with a child may grow up to be a dog that is shy around or aggressive toward children.

CONSISTENCY IN TRAINING
Dogs, being pack animals, naturally need a leader, or else they try to establish dominance in their packs. When you welcome a dog into your family, the choice of who becomes the leader and who becomes the "pack" is entirely up to you! Your pup's intuitive quest for dominance, coupled with the fact that it is nearly impossible to look at an adorable Anatolian pup with his puppy-dog eyes and not cave in, give the pup almost an unfair advantage in getting the upper hand! A pup will definitely test the waters to see what he can and cannot do. Do not give in to that pleading expression—stand your ground when it comes to disciplining the pup and make sure that all family members do the same. It will only confuse the pup if Mother tells him to get off the sofa when he is used to sitting up there with Father to watch the

MANNERS MATTER
During the socialization process, a puppy should meet people, experience different environments and definitely be exposed to other canines. Through playing and interacting with other dogs, your puppy will learn lessons, ranging from controlling the pressure of his jaws by biting his littermates to the inner workings of the canine pack that he will apply to his human relationships for the rest of his life. That is why removing a puppy from his litter too early (before eight weeks) can be detrimental to the pup's development.

SOCIALIZATION

Thorough socialization includes not only meeting new people but also being introduced to new experiences such as riding in the car, having his coat brushed, hearing the television, walking in a crowd—the list is endless. The more your pup experiences, and the more positive the experiences are, the less of a shock and the less frightening it will be for your pup to encounter new things.

nightly news. Avoid discrepancies by having all members of the household decide on the rules before the pup even comes home…and be consistent in enforcing them! Early training shapes the dog's personality, so you cannot be unclear in what you expect.

COMMON PUPPY PROBLEMS

The best way to prevent puppy problems is to be proactive in stopping an undesirable behavior as soon as it starts. The old saying "You can't teach an old dog new tricks" does not necessarily hold true, but it is true that it is much easier to discourage bad behavior in a young developing pup than to wait until the pup's bad behavior becomes the adult dog's bad habit. There are some problems that are especially prevalent in puppies as they develop.

NIPPING

As puppies start to teethe, they feel the need to sink their teeth into anything available…unfortunately, that usually includes your fingers, arms, hair and toes. You may find this behavior cute for the first five seconds…until you feel just how sharp those puppy teeth are. Nipping is something you

PROPER SOCIALIZATION

The socialization period for puppies is from age 8 to 16 weeks. This is the time when puppies need to leave their birth family and take up residence with their new owners, where they will meet many new people, other pets, etc. Failure to be adequately socialized can cause the dog to grow up fearing others and being shy and unfriendly due to a lack of self-confidence.

CRYING/WHINING

Your pup will often cry, whine, whimper, howl or make some type of commotion when he is left alone. This is basically his way of calling out for attention to make sure that you know he is there and that you have not forgotten about him. Your puppy feels insecure when he is left alone, when you are out of the house and he is in his crate or when you are in another part of the house and he cannot see you. The noise he is making is an expression of the anxiety he feels at being alone, so he needs to be taught that being alone is okay. You are not actually training the dog to stop making noise; rather, you are training him to feel comfortable when he is alone and thus removing the need for him to make the noise.

This is where the crate with cozy bedding and a toy comes in handy. You want to know that

Nipping and chewing go along with being a puppy, and whatever soothes his growing teeth and sore gums will likely find its way into his mouth.

want to discourage immediately and consistently with a firm "No!" (or whatever number of firm "Nos" it takes for him to understand that you mean business). Then, replace your finger with an appropriate chew toy. While this behavior is merely annoying when the dog is young, it can become dangerous as your Anatolian's adult teeth grow in and his jaws develop, and he continues to think it is okay to gnaw on human appendages. Your Anatolian does not mean any harm with a friendly nip, but he also does not know his own strength.

IN DUE TIME
It will take at least two weeks for your puppy to become accustomed to his new surroundings. Give him lots of love, attention, handling, frequent opportunities to relieve himself, a diet he likes to eat and a place he can call his own.

CHEWING TIPS

Chewing goes hand in hand with nipping in the sense that a teething puppy is always looking for a way to soothe his aching gums. In this case, instead of chewing on you, he may have taken a liking to your favorite shoe or something else that he should not be chewing. Again, realize that this is a normal canine behavior that does not need to be discouraged, only redirected. Your pup just needs to be taught what is acceptable to chew on and what is off-limits. Consistently tell him "No!" when you catch him chewing on something forbidden and give him a chew toy.

Conversely, praise him when you catch him chewing on something appropriate. In this way, you are discouraging the inappropriate behavior and reinforcing the desired behavior. The puppy's chewing should stop after his adult teeth have come in, but an adult dog continues to chew for various reasons—perhaps because he is bored, needs to relieve tension or just likes to chew. That is why it is important to redirect his chewing when he is still young.

your pup is safe when you are not there to supervise, and you know that he will be safe in his crate rather than roaming freely about the house. In order for the pup to stay in his crate without making a fuss, he first needs to be comfortable in his crate. On that note, it is extremely important that the crate is never used as a form of punishment; this will cause the pup to view the crate as a negative place, rather than as a place of his own for safety and retreat.

Accustom the pup to the crate in short, gradually increasing time intervals in which you put him in the crate, maybe with a treat, and stay in the room with him. If he cries or makes a fuss, do not go to him, but stay in his sight. Gradually he will realize that staying in his crate is okay without your help, and it will not be so traumatic for him when you are not around. You may want to leave the radio on softly when you leave the house; the sound of human voices may be comforting to him.

"Where did everybody go?" A small pup can make a big noise when he needs security and attention.

EVERYDAY CARE OF YOUR
ANATOLIAN
SHEPHERD DOG

SPECIAL FEEDING RECOMMENDATIONS

Every Anatolian breeder should have his own tried-and-true method of feeding. Before your puppy leaves the breeder's home or kennel, you can rest assured that you will depart with careful instructions on how to follow the breeder's established feeding program. In the highly unlikely case of the breeder's not automatically providing you with this information, do not leave without asking for it.

What and when you should feed your new puppy will be included in the diet sheet and it is important to understand that a specific feeding schedule is important to the puppy's well-being. A good rule of thumb for establishing intake is the amount of food the puppy, or adult for that matter, will eat in five minutes. The recommended content may vary from breeder to breeder, but the five-minute rule is apt to remain constant.

Unlike the advice given to the new owners of many other breeds, the Anatolian's food intake must be regulated carefully because growing Anatolians have ravenous appetites and too much food can result in an overweight puppy. This puts undue stress on the

STORING DOG FOOD

You must store your dry dog food carefully. Open packages of dog food quickly lose their vitamin value, usually within 90 days of being opened. Mold spores and vermin could also contaminate the food.

puppy's skeletal development.

Over-supplementation and forced growth are now looked upon by many breeders as major contributors to the high incidence of skeletal abnormalities and chronic skin conditions found in many pure-bred dogs of the day. Some people may claim these problems are entirely hereditary but most others feel they can, if nothing more, be exacerbated by diet and over-use of mineral and vitamin supplements for puppies.

When feeding a commercially prepared dog food, no growth supplements should be added to the Anatolian puppy's diet, as all leading major-brand dog foods are highly fortified and should contain all the nutrients your dog requires. Supplementation can create an excess of certain nutrients already contained in the food, which can cause nutritional imbalances and both skeletal and joint deformities.

After weaning and on up to about three months, the Anatolian puppy should be getting three to four meals a day. At that point,

The breeder introduces milk meals as a part of the weaning process.

two to three meals a day are sufficient; by the time the puppy is six months old, he might well be put on a morning/evening schedule. Here again, these are simply rules of thumb. The lean and leggy puppy might need an additional feeding along with the morning/evening schedule. The too-pudgy puppy should be kept on the two-meal schedule but perhaps be given a bit less at each.

Most commercial foods manufactured for dogs meet nutrition standards and list the ingredients contained in the food on every package and container. The ingredients are listed in descending order with the main ingredient listed first. Some breeders do not feel that commercial complete diets are suitable for the Anatolian. One breeder even feeds her dogs whole chicken carcasses—something not recommended for most other

TEST FOR PROPER DIET

A good test for proper diet is the color, odor and firmness of your dog's stool. A healthy dog usually produces three semi-hard stools per day. The stools should have no unpleasant odor. They should be the same color from excretion to excretion.

Feeding time! Anatolians love to eat, and this group of youngsters eagerly follows the breeder with their eyes on the dinner bowl.

breeds! Use your breeder's experience and advice as a guide in selecting the best diet for your Anatolian.

Refined sugars are not a part of a canine's natural food acquisition, and canine teeth are not genetically disposed to handling these sugars. Do not feed your Anatolian sugar products and avoid products that contain sugar in any high degree.

Fresh water and a properly prepared, balanced diet that contains the essential nutrients in correct proportions are all a healthy Anatolian needs to be offered. Dog foods come canned, dry, semi-moist, "scientifically fortified" and "all-natural." A visit to your local market or pet store will reveal how vast an array you will be able to select from.

All dogs, whether large or small, are carnivorous (meat-eating) animals. Animal protein and fats are essential to the well-being of your Anatolian. However, a diet too high in proteins can lead to problems as well. Not all dry foods contain the correct amount of protein for the Anatolian's well-being. If protein supplementation is needed, a protein source other than red meat (like chicken) should be fed to the Anatolian. It is best to discuss this with the breeder from whom you purchase your dog or with your vet. The domesticated dog's diet must include protein,

FOOD PREFERENCE

Selecting the best dry dog food is difficult. There is no majority consensus among veterinary scientists as to the value of nutrient analysis (protein, fat, fiber, moisture, ash, cholesterol, minerals, etc.). All agree that feeding trials are what matter most, but you also have to consider the individual dog. The dog's weight, age and activity level, and what pleases his taste, all must be considered. It is probably best to take the advice of your veterinarian. Every dog's dietary requirements vary, even during the lifetime of a particular dog.

Consult your veterinarian and/or breeder regarding supplements of meat or vegetables. Dogs do appreciate a little variety in their diets, so you may choose to vary the flavor of the dry food you feed. Alternatively, you may wish to add a little flavored stock to give a difference to the taste.

carbohydrates, fats, roughage and small amounts of minerals and vitamins. Many breeders strongly recommend adding small amounts of cooked vegetables to an Anatolian's diet. This provides the necessary carbohydrates, minerals and nutrients present only in vegetables.

EXERCISE

If a breed's exercise requirements were in direct proportion to its size, one would expect the Anatolian's requirements to appear at the very top of the list. Quite the contrary is actually true—at least in adulthood. Like any youngster, the growing Anatolian will have bursts of excited energy and then there will be long periods of rest to re-energize. But as the Anatolian matures, his exercise needs decrease markedly.

Inexperienced Anatolian owners sometimes wonder if there is something wrong with their grown dog because he seems almost comatose at times. Their fears are quickly relieved, however, with the arrival of an intruder, whether man or beast. The seemingly sound-asleep Anatolian is suddenly on his feet and leaping into action. You could say that the Anatolian's sense of hearing never sleeps. That sense is so highly developed that many of us who really know the Anatolian are convinced the breed is able to hear things before they actually happen.

All this is to say that your Anatolian will do a pretty good job of exercising himself, given the properly enclosed area to do so. If your Anatolian is living with another dog, the two will undoubtedly devise some games to play early in the day or late in the evening when temperatures are ideal for such activity.

Don't think your Anatolian is unable to exercise, though. If you need a hiking partner, there's no better dog to take along. An Anatolian can go as far as you can

TIPPING THE SCALES
Good nutrition is vital to your dog's health, but many people end up over-feeding or giving unnecessary supplements. Here are some common doggie diet don'ts:
• Adding milk, yogurt and cheese to your dog's diet may seem like a good idea for coat and skin care, but dairy products are very fattening and can cause indigestion.
• Diets high in fat will not cause heart attacks in dogs but will certainly cause your dog to gain weight.
• Most importantly, don't assume your dog will simply stop eating once he doesn't need any more food. Given the chance, he will eat you out of house and home!

and further! And you can rest assured that no one is going to bother you along the way!

Mature Anatolians are capable and willing jogging companions. It is important, however, to use good judgment in any exercise program. Begin slowly and increase the distance to be covered very gradually over an extended period of time. Use special precautions in hot weather. High temperatures and forced exercise are a dangerous combination, but it is highly doubtful that you will be able to get your Anatolian to risk his health in that way. The breed has too great a history of using good sense in whatever is attempted.

Needless to say, puppies should never be forced to exercise. Normally, they are little dynamos of energy and keep themselves busy all day long, interspersed with frequent naps. The Anatolian puppy should not be given vigorous exercise until after six months of age.

GROOMING

COAT MAINTENANCE
The Anatolian is a natural breed that requires no fancy clipping or trimming. In fact, you don't even have to own a pair of scissors to groom this breed. You do need a good strong slicker or pin brush and a good natural bristle brush that has some nylon bristles

inserted in it. You will also need a steel comb to remove any debris that collects in the longer furnishings. A comb that has teeth divided between fine and coarse is ideal. All of these supplies are available at the local pet shop.

Regular thorough brushing with the slicker or pin brush helps keep the hair deposits on your carpeting and furniture down to a minimum. This procedure becomes an absolute necessity during those twice-a-year seasonal coat sheddings. There's no need to tell you what times of the year your Anatolian will blow his coat. Your regular brushing will tell you that in a hurry. Or, if you fall behind on your brushing chores, the clouds of coat floating through the house will quickly inform you.

When brushing, proceed vigorously from behind the head

Do you have enough space for your Anatolian to run? Is your yard securely fenced? Do you have time to spend with your Anatolian, participating in different endeavors to keep him active and interested?

The times when your Anatolian is shedding will be quite obvious. More frequent brushing during these times will remove the dead hair and collect it in the brush rather than on your clothes, carpets and furniture.

to the tail. Do this all over the body and be especially careful to attend to the hard-to-reach areas between the legs, behind the ears and under the body. Mats can occur, particularly when the dog is shedding or when the coat catches burrs or sticky substances in the longer furnishings.

Should you encounter a mat that does not brush out easily, use your fingers and the steel comb to separate the hairs as much as possible. Do not cut or pull out the matted hair. Apply baby powder or one of the specially prepared grooming powders directly to the mat and brush completely from the skin out.

Follow your slicker or pin brushing with a stimulating once-over with the bristle brush. Together, these will keep both the coat and skin clean and healthy.

You can dry-bathe your Anatolian by sprinkling a little baby powder in the coat and then working it well in and brushing it out. This, of course, also helps to make the dog smell good.

Over-bathing can lead to dry skin problems. Dry skin creates a need to scratch and this can lead to severe scratching and hot spots, moist sore areas in which the coat is entirely scratched away.

NAIL TRIMMING AND FOOT CARE

This is a good time to accustom your Anatolian to having his nails trimmed and feet inspected.

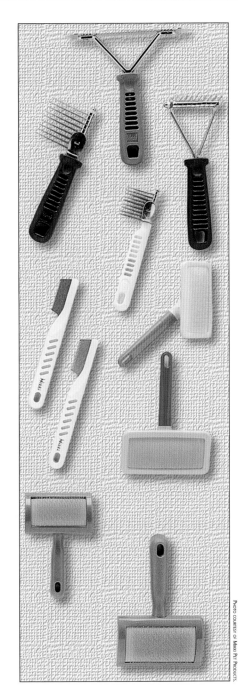

The Anatolian does not require specialized grooming. You should be able to find all of the basic grooming tools for maintaining your dog's coat wherever you buy pet supplies.

PHOTO COURTESY OF MIKKI PET PRODUCTS.

Use the slicker brush to carefully brush through your Anatolian's coat.

An undercoat rake will be useful in removing dead hairs that can accumulate in the coat during shedding times.

The ears can be cleaned with a soft wipe and ear cleaner. Never probe into the dog's ear canal.

Accustoming your Anatolian to grooming (or anything else, for that matter) as a puppy is an excellent idea. Trying to convince the large adult to be still for brushing if he has never experienced it before can be a considerable chore.

Nail Maintenance

Nail Casing

Quick

Cut Line

Dark-Colored Nails

With black or dark nails, it's best to clip only the tip of the nail or to use a file or drummel.

Light-Colored Nails

In light-colored nails, clipping is much simpler because you can see the vein (or quick) that grows inside the casing.

Always inspect your dog's feet for cracked pads. Check between the toes for splinters and thorns that may be embedded in the soft hair between the pads and toes. Pay particular attention to any swollen or tender areas.

I suggest attending to your dog's nails at intervals of at least every three weeks and certainly no longer than four weeks. Long nails spread and weaken the foot. The nails of an Anatolian that isn't exercising on rough terrain will grow long very quickly.

Each nail has a blood vessel running through the center called the "quick." The quick grows close to the end of the nail and contains very sensitive nerve endings. If the nail is allowed to grow too long, it will be impossible to cut it back to a proper length without cutting into the quick. This causes severe pain to the dog and can also result in a great deal of bleeding that can be very difficult to stop.

Nails can be trimmed with canine nail clippers or an electric nail grinder called a drummel. Use the "fine" grinding disc on the drummel because this allows you to trim back the nail a little bit at a time, usually avoiding any bleeding.

Always proceed with caution and remove only a small portion of the nail at a time. Should the quick be nipped in the trimming process, there are any number of blood-clotting products available

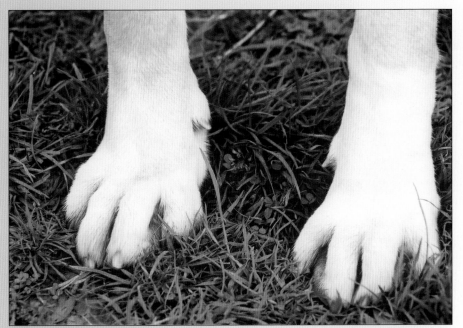

Good front feet of an adult bitch, with neatly trimmed nails.

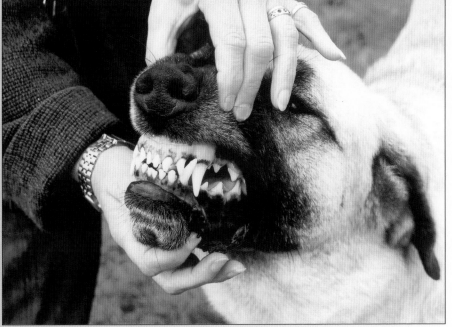

Your Anatolian has a strong, husky set of teeth. A home dental-care routine, including routine checkups and regular tooth-brushing, will help them stay white and healthy.

Your Anatolian should be comfortable during grooming. This dog prefers to lie on his back during his pedicure, and this gives his owner easy access to his feet.

at pet shops that will almost immediately stem the flow of blood. You can also use a styptic pencil, such as the one used for shaving. It is wise to have one of these products on hand anyway in case your dog breaks a nail in some way.

TRAVELING WITH YOUR DOG

CAR TRAVEL

You should accustom your Anatolian to riding in a car at an early age. You may or may not take him in the car often, but at the very least he will need to go to the vet and you do not want these trips to be traumatic for the dog or troublesome for you. The safest way for a dog to ride in the car is in his crate. If he uses a crate in the house, you can use the same

crate for travel. If you are fortunate enough to own a vehicle large enough to accommodate your Anatolian's crate, then that is your safest option.

Another option for car travel is a specially made safety harness for dogs, which straps the dog in much like a seat belt. Do not let the dog roam loose in the vehicle—this is very dangerous! If

TRAVEL SAFELY

The most extensive travel you do with your dog may be limited to trips to the veterinarian's office—or you may decide to bring him along for long distances when the family goes on vacation. Whichever the case, it is important to consider your dog's safety while traveling.

you should stop short, your dog can be thrown and injured. If the dog starts climbing on you and pestering you while you are driving, you will not be able to concentrate on the road. It is an unsafe situation for everyone—human and canine.

For long trips, be prepared to stop to let the dog relieve himself. Take with you whatever you need to clean up after him, including some paper towels and perhaps some old bath towels for use should he have a "bathroom" accident in the car or suffer from motion sickness.

AIR TRAVEL

Contact your chosen airline before proceeding with your travel plans that include your Anatolian. The dog will be required to travel in a fiberglass crate and you should always check in advance with the airline regarding specific requirements for the crate's size, type and labeling. To help put the dog at ease, give him one of his favorite toys in the crate. Do not feed the dog for several hours before checking in, in order to minimize his need to relieve himself. However, depending on the length of the flight, certain regulations specify that food, water and bowls must be attached to the outside of the crate.

Make sure your dog is properly identified and that your contact information appears on

TRAVEL CAUTION!
Never leave your dog alone in the car. In hot weather, your dog can die from the high temperature inside a closed vehicle; even a car parked in the shade can heat up very quickly. Leaving the window open is dangerous as well since the dog can hurt himself trying to get out.

Should you decide not to take your Anatolian away with you, he can be boarded at a suitable kennel. The kennel should be clean, of adequate size for large-breed dogs and staffed by knowledgeable professionals. Your vet can probably recommend a suitable kennel facility.

his ID tags and on his crate. Animals travel in a different area of the plane than human passengers, so every rule must be strictly followed so as to prevent the risk of getting separated from your dog.

BOARDING

So you want to take a family outing—and you want to include *all* members of the family. You would probably make arrangements for accommodations ahead of time anyway, but this is especially important when traveling with a dog. You do not want to make an overnight stop at the only place around for miles,

only to find out that they do not allow dogs. Also, you do not want to reserve a place for your family without confirming that you are traveling with a dog, because, if it is against their policy, you may end up without a place to stay.

Alternatively, if you are traveling and choose not to bring your Anatolian, you will have to make arrangements for him while you are away. Some options are to take him to a neighbor's house to stay while you are gone, to have a trusted and familiar neighbor stay at your house or to bring your dog to a reputable boarding kennel. If you choose to board him at a kennel, you should visit in

IDENTIFICATION OPTIONS

As puppies become more and more expensive, especially those puppies of high quality for showing and/or breeding, they have a greater chance of being stolen. The usual collar is, of course, easily removed. But there are two more permanent techniques that have become widely used for identification.

The puppy microchip implantation involves the injection of a small microchip, about the size of a grain of uncooked rice, under the skin of the dog. If your dog shows up at a clinic or shelter, or is offered for resale under less-than-savory circumstances, he can be positively identified by the microchip. The microchip is scanned, and a registry quickly identifies you as the owner.

Tattooing is done on various parts of the dog, from his belly to his cheeks. The number tattooed can be your telephone number or any other number that you can easily memorize. When professional dog thieves see a tattooed dog, they usually lose interest. For the safety of our dogs, no laboratory facility or dog broker will accept a tattooed dog as stock. Both microchipping and tattooing can be done at your local veterinary clinic.

advance to see the facilities provided and where the dogs are kept. Are the dogs' areas spacious and kept clean? Talk to some of the employees and observe how they treat the dogs—do they spend time with the dogs, play with them, exercise them, etc.? Also find out the kennel's policy on vaccinations and what they require. This is for all of the dogs' safety, since there is a greater risk of diseases being passed from dog to dog when dogs are kept together.

IDENTIFICATION

Your Anatolian is your valued companion and friend. That is why you always keep a close eye on him and you have made sure that he cannot escape from your property or wriggle out of his collar and run away from you. However, accidents can happen and there may come a time when your dog unexpectedly becomes separated from you. If this unfortunate event should occur, the first thing on your mind will be finding him. Proper identification, including an ID tag, a tattoo and possibly a microchip, will increase the chances of his being returned to you safely and quickly.

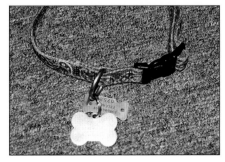

Proper identification tags are a simple way to help ensure your dog's return should he wander away from home.

The time spent training your Anatolian Shepherd is essential to building the bond between a well-behaved dog and a happy owner.

TRAINING YOUR
ANATOLIAN SHEPHERD DOG

Living with an untrained dog is a lot like owning a piano that you do not know how to play—it is a nice object to look at, but it does not do much more than that to bring you pleasure. Now try taking piano lessons, and suddenly the piano comes alive and brings forth magical sounds and rhythms that set your heart singing and your body swaying.

The same is true with your Anatolian Shepherd Dog. Any dog is a big responsibility and, if not trained sensibly, may develop unacceptable behavior that annoys you or could even cause family friction. With a dog as large as the Anatolian, the owner's responsibility to train him is considerably increased. An untrained Anatolian Shepherd can be an unruly, dangerous animal that poses a threat to you or others around you.

To train your Anatolian, you may like to enroll in an obedience class. Teach your dog good manners as you learn how and why he behaves the way he does. Find out how to communicate with your dog and how to recognize and understand his communications with you. Suddenly the dog takes on a new role in your life—he is clever, interesting, well behaved and fun to be with. He demonstrates his bond of devotion to you daily. In other words, your Anatolian does wonders for your ego because he constantly reminds you that you are not only his leader you are also his hero!

Those involved with teaching dog obedience and counseling owners about their dogs' behavior have discovered some interesting facts about dog ownership. For example, training dogs when they are puppies results in the highest rate of success in developing well-mannered and well-adjusted adult

REAP THE REWARDS

If you start with a normal, healthy dog and give him time, patience and some carefully executed lessons, you will reap the rewards of that training for the life of the dog. And what a life it will be! The two of you will find immeasurable pleasure in the companionship you have built together with love, respect and understanding.

dogs. Training an older dog, from six months to six years of age, can produce almost equal results, providing that the owner accepts the dog's slower rate of learning capability and is willing to work patiently to help the dog succeed at developing to his fullest potential. Unfortunately, many owners of untrained adult dogs lack the patience factor, so they do not persist until their dogs are successful at learning particular behaviors.

Training a puppy aged 10 to 16 weeks (20 weeks at the most) is like working with a dry sponge in a pool of water. The pup soaks up whatever you show him and constantly looks for more things to do and learn. At this early age, his body is not yet producing hormones, and therein lies the reason for such a high rate of success. Without hormones, he is focused on his owners and not particularly interested in investigating other places, dogs, people, etc. You are his leader: his provider of food, water, shelter and security. He latches onto you and wants to stay close. He will usually follow you from room to room, will not let you out of his sight when you are outdoors with him and will respond in like manner to the people and animals you encounter. If you greet a friend warmly, he will be happy to greet the person as well. If, however, you are hesitant or

FEAR AGGRESSION

Pups who are subjected to physical abuse during training commonly end up with behavioral problems as adults. One common result of abuse is fear aggression, in which a dog will lash out, bare his teeth, snarl and finally bite someone by whom he feels threatened. For example, your daughter may be playing with the dog one afternoon. As they play hide-and-seek, she backs the dog into a corner and, as she attempts to tease him playfully, he bites her hand. Examine the cause of this behavior. Did your daughter ever hit the dog? Did someone who resembles your daughter hit or scream at the dog?

Fortunately, fear aggression is relatively easy to correct. Have your daughter engage in only positive activities with the dog, such as feeding, petting and walking. She should not give any corrections or negative feedback. If the dog still growls or cowers away from her, allow someone else to accompany them. After approximately one week, the dog should feel that he can rely on her for many positive things, and he will also be prevented from reacting fearfully towards anyone who might resemble her.

anxious about the approach of a stranger, he will respond accordingly.

Once the puppy begins to produce hormones, his natural curiosity emerges and he begins to investigate the world around him. It is at this time when you may notice that the untrained dog begins to wander away from you and even ignore your commands to stay close. When this behavior becomes a problem, you have two choices: get rid of the dog or train him. It is strongly urged that you choose the latter option.

You usually will be able to find obedience classes within a reasonable distance from your home, but you can also do a lot to train your dog yourself. Sometimes there are classes available, but the tuition is too costly. Whatever the circumstances, the

Energetic pups have a lot on their young minds other than training, so you'll have to be creative in focusing their attention on the basic lessons that should begin in puppyhood.

solution to training your dog without formal obedience lessons lies within the pages of this book.

This chapter is devoted to helping you train your Anatolian at home. If the recommended procedures are followed faithfully, you may expect positive results that will prove rewarding both to you and your dog.

Whether your new charge is a puppy or a mature adult, the methods of teaching and the techniques we use in training

SAFETY FIRST
While it may seem that the most important things to your dog are eating, sleeping and chewing the upholstery on your furniture, his first concern is actually safety. The domesticated dogs we keep as companions have the same pack instinct as their ancestors who ran free thousands of years ago. Because of this pack instinct, your dog wants to know that he and his pack are not in danger of being harmed, and that his pack has a strong, capable leader. You must establish yourself as the leader early on in your relationship. That way your dog will trust that you will take care of him and the pack, and he will accept your commands without question.

PARENTAL GUIDANCE
Training a dog is a life experience. Many parents admit that much of what they know about raising children they learned from caring for their dogs. Dogs respond to love, fairness and guidance, just as children do. Become a good dog owner and you may become an even better parent.

basic behaviors are the same. After all, no dog, whether puppy or adult, likes harsh or inhumane methods. All creatures, however, respond favorably to gentle motivational methods and sincere praise and encouragement. Now let us get started.

HOUSE-TRAINING
You can train a puppy to relieve himself wherever you choose, but this must be somewhere suitable. You should bear in mind from the outset that when your puppy is old enough to go out in public places, any canine deposits must be removed at once. You will always have to carry with you a small plastic bag or "poop-scoop."

Outdoor training includes such surfaces as grass, soil and cement. Indoor training usually means training your dog to newspaper. When deciding on the surface and location that you will want your Anatolian to use, be sure it is going to be permanent. Training your dog to grass and then changing your mind a few months later is extremely difficult for both dog and owner.

Next, choose the command you will use each and every time you want your puppy to void. "Hurry up" and "Let's go" are examples of commands commonly used by dog owners. Get in the habit of giving the puppy your chosen relief command before you take him out. That way, when he

HONOR AND OBEY
Dogs are the most honorable animals in existence. They consider another species (humans) as their own. They interface with you. You are their leader. Puppies perceive children to be on their level; their actions around small children are different from their behavior around their adult masters.

becomes an adult, you will be able to determine if he wants to go out when you ask him. A confirmation will be signs of interest such as wagging his tail, watching you intently, going to the door, etc.

PUPPY'S NEEDS
The puppy needs to relieve himself after play periods, after each meal, after he has been sleeping and at any time he indicates that he is looking for a place to urinate or defecate. The urinary and intestinal tract muscles of very young puppies

THINK BEFORE YOU BARK
Dogs are sensitive to their masters' moods and emotions. Use your voice wisely when communicating with your dog. Never raise your voice at your dog unless you are angry and trying to correct him. "Barking" at your dog can become as meaningless as "dogspeak" is to you.

CANINE DEVELOPMENT SCHEDULE

It is important to understand how and at what age a puppy develops into adulthood.
If you are a puppy owner, consult the following Canine Development Schedule to
determine the stage of development your puppy is currently experiencing.
This knowledge will help you as you work with the puppy in the weeks and months ahead.

Period	Age	Characteristics
FIRST TO THIRD	BIRTH TO SEVEN WEEKS	Puppy needs food, sleep and warmth, and responds to simple and gentle touching. Needs mother for security and disciplining. Needs littermates for learning and interacting with other dogs. Pup learns to function within a pack and learns pack order of dominance. Begin socializing with adults and children for short periods. Begins to become aware of his environment.
FOURTH	EIGHT TO TWELVE WEEKS	Brain is fully developed. Needs socializing with outside world. Remove from mother and littermates. Needs to change from canine pack to human pack. Human dominance necessary. Fear period occurs between 8 and 12 weeks. Avoid fright and pain.
FIFTH	THIRTEEN TO SIXTEEN WEEKS	Training and formal obedience should begin. Less association with other dogs, more with people, places, situations. Period will pass easily if you remember this is pup's change-to-adolescence time. Be firm and fair. Flight instinct prominent. Permissiveness and over-disciplining can do permanent damage. Praise for good behavior.
JUVENILE	FOUR TO EIGHT MONTHS	Another fear period about 7 to 8 months of age. It passes quickly, but be cautious of fright and pain. Sexual maturity reached. Dominant traits established. Dog should understand sit, down, come and stay by now.

NOTE: THESE ARE APPROXIMATE TIME FRAMES. ALLOW FOR INDIVIDUAL DIFFERENCES IN PUPPIES.

Dogs have very strong scenting abilities and use their noses for many things, including locating their relief areas and investigating visits from other dogs.

are not fully developed. Therefore, like human babies, puppies need to relieve themselves frequently.

Take your puppy out often—every hour for an eight-week-old, for example—and always immediately after sleeping and eating. The older the puppy, the less often he will need to relieve himself. Finally, as a mature healthy adult, he will require only three to five relief trips per day.

HOUSING

Since the types of housing and control you provide for your puppy have a direct relationship on the success of house-training, we consider the various aspects of both before we begin training.

Taking a new puppy home and turning him loose in your house can be compared to turning a child loose in a sports arena and telling the child that the place is all his! The sheer enormity of the place would be too much for him to handle. Instead, offer the puppy clearly defined areas where he can play, sleep, eat and live. A room of the house where the family gathers is the most obvious choice. Puppies are social animals and need to feel a part of the pack right from the start. Hearing your voice, watching you while you are doing things and smelling you nearby are all positive reinforcers that he is now a member of your pack. Usually a family room, the kitchen or a nearby adjoining breakfast area is ideal for providing safety and security for both puppy and owner.

Within the designated room, there should be a smaller area that

PRACTICE MAKES PERFECT!

- Have training lessons with your dog every day in several short segments—three to five times a day for a few minutes at a time is ideal.
- Do not have long practice sessions. The dog will become easily bored.
- Never practice when you are tired, ill, worried or in an otherwise negative mood. This will transmit to the dog and may have an adverse effect on his performance.

Think fun, short and above all positive! End each session on a high note, rather than a failed exercise, and make sure to give a lot of praise. Enjoy the training and help your dog enjoy it, too.

MEALTIME

Mealtime should be a peaceful time for your puppy. Do not put his food and water bowls in a high-traffic area in the house. For example, give him his own little corner of the kitchen where he can eat undisturbed and where he will not be underfoot. Do not allow small children or other family members to disturb the pup when he is eating.

the puppy can call his own. An alcove, a wire or fiberglass dog crate or a fenced (not boarded!) corner from which he can view the activities of his new family will be fine. The size of the area or crate is the key factor here. The area must be large enough so that the puppy can lie down and stretch out, as well as stand up, without rubbing his head on the top. At the same time, it must be small enough so that he cannot relieve himself at one end and sleep at the other without coming into contact with his droppings before he is fully trained to relieve himself outside. Dogs are, by nature, clean animals and will not remain close to their relief areas unless forced to do so. In those cases, they then become dirty dogs and usually remain that way for life.

The dog's designated area should contain clean bedding and a toy. Water must always be available, in a non-spill container;

this can be put in the dog's crate or area once house-training has been achieved reliably.

CONTROL

By control, we mean helping the puppy to create a lifestyle pattern that will be compatible to that of his human pack (YOU!). Just as we guide little children to learn our way of life, we must show the puppy when it is time to play, eat, sleep, exercise and even entertain himself.

Imagine the breeder's challenge in raising a litter of rapidly growing Anatolians. This young bunch is attentive to following their leader.

Your puppy should always take his naps in his crate. He should also learn that, during times of household confusion and excessive human activity, such as at breakfast when family members are preparing for the day, he can play by himself in relative safety and comfort in his designated area. Each time you leave the puppy alone, he should understand exactly where he is to stay.

Puppies are chewers. They cannot tell the difference between lamp cords, television wires, shoes, table legs, etc. Chewing into a television wire, for example, can be fatal to the puppy, while a shorted wire can start a fire in the house. If the puppy, chews on the arm of the chair when he is alone, you will probably discipline him angrily when you get home. Thus, he makes the association that your coming home means he is going to

THE SUCCESS METHOD

6 Steps to Successful Crate Training

1 Tell the puppy "Crate time!" and place him in the crate with a small treat (a piece of cheese or half of a biscuit). Let him stay in the crate for 5 minutes while you are in the same room. Then release him and praise lavishly. Never release him when he is fussing. Wait until he is quiet before you let him out.

2 Repeat Step 1 several times a day.

3 The next day, place the puppy in the crate as before. Let him stay there for ten minutes. Do this several times.

4 Continue building time in 5-minute increments until the puppy stays in his crate for 30 minutes with you in the room. Always take him to his relief area after prolonged periods in his crate.

5 Now go back to Step 1 and let the puppy stay in his crate for five minutes, this time while you are out of the room.

6 Once again, build crate time in 5-minute increments with you out of the room. When the puppy will stay willingly in his crate (he may even fall asleep!) for 30 minutes with you out of the room, he will be ready to stay in it for several hours at a time.

be punished. (He will not remember chewing the chair and is incapable of making the association of the discipline with his naughty deed.) Accustoming the pup to his designated area not only keeps him safe but also avoids his engaging in destructive behaviors when you are not around.

Times of excitement, such as special occasions, family parties, etc., can be fun for the puppy, providing that he can view the activities from the security of his designated area. He is not

HOW MANY TIMES A DAY?

AGE	RELIEF TRIPS
To 14 weeks	10
14–22 weeks	8
22–32 weeks	6
Adulthood	4
(dog stops growing)	

These are estimates, of course, but they are a guide to the *minimum* number of opportunities a dog should have each day to relieve himself.

underfoot and he is not being fed all sorts of tidbits that will probably cause him stomach distress, yet he still feels a part of the fun.

SCHEDULE

A puppy should be taken to his relief area each time he is released from his designated area, after meals, after play sessions and when he first awakens in the morning (at age eight weeks, this can mean 5 a.m.!). The puppy will indicate that he's ready "to go" by circling or sniffing busily—do not misinterpret these signs. For a puppy less than ten weeks of age, a routine of taking him out every hour is necessary. As the puppy grows, he will be able to wait for longer periods of time.

Keep trips to his relief area short. Stay no more than five or six minutes and then return to the house. If he goes during that time, praise him lavishly and take him indoors immediately. If he does not, but he has an accident when you go back indoors, pick him up immediately, say "No! No!" and return to his relief area. Wait a few minutes, then return to the house again. Never hit a puppy or put his face in urine or excrement when he has had an accident!

Once indoors, put the puppy in his crate until you have had time to clean up his accident. Then, release him to the family area and watch him more closely

---

HOUSE-TRAINING TIP

Most of all, be consistent. Always take your dog to the same location, always use the same command and always have the dog on lead when he is in his relief area, or within a fenced-in yard.

By following the Success Method, your puppy will be completely house-trained by the time his muscle and brain development reach maturity. Keep in mind that large breeds mature more slowly than small breeds, but all puppies should be trained by six months of age.

---

than before. Chances are, his accident was a result of your not picking up his signal or waiting too long before offering him the opportunity to relieve himself. Never hold a grudge against the puppy for accidents.

Let the puppy learn that going outdoors means it is time to relieve himself, not to play. Once trained, he will be able to play indoors and out and still differentiate between the times for play versus the times for relief.

Help him develop regular hours for naps, being alone, playing by himself and just resting, all in his crate, though never for more than an hour or two. Encourage him to entertain himself while you are busy with your activities. Let him learn that having you near is comforting, but

---

CALM DOWN

Dogs will do anything for your attention. If you reward the dog when he is calm and attentive, you will develop a well-mannered dog. If, on the other hand, you greet your dog excitedly and encourage him to wrestle with you, the dog will greet you the same way and you will have a hyperactive dog on your hands.

Your fenced-in yard is the ideal relief site for your Anatolian, as you can choose an out-of-the-way spot and train him to always use the same area.

The crate you select should be able to comfortably house an adult Anatolian. Therefore, get the adult-size crate as soon as you acquire the puppy and accustom him to it from puppyhood.

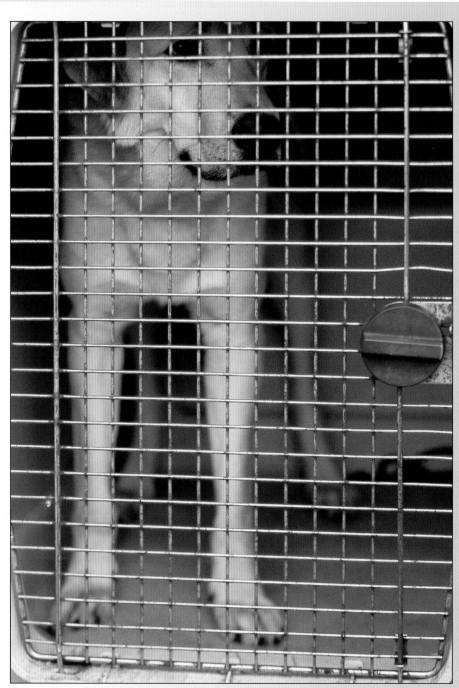

it is not your main purpose in life to provide him with undivided attention.

Each time you put your puppy in his own area, use the same command, whatever suits best. Soon he will run to his crate or special area when he hears you say those words.

Crate training provides safety for you, the puppy and the home. It also provides the puppy with a feeling of security, and that helps the puppy achieve self-confidence and clean habits. Remember that one of the primary ingredients in house-training your puppy is control. Regardless of your lifestyle, there will always be occasions when you will need to have a place where your dog can stay and be happy and safe. Crate training is the answer for now and in the future.

In conclusion, a few key elements are really all you need for a successful house-training method—consistency, frequency, praise, control and supervision. By following these procedures with a normal, healthy puppy, you and the puppy will soon be past the stage of accidents and ready to move on to a full and rewarding life together.

ROLES OF DISCIPLINE, REWARD AND PUNISHMENT
Discipline, training one to act in accordance with rules, brings order to life. It is as simple as that. Without discipline, particularly in a group society, chaos will reign supreme and the group will eventually perish. Humans and canines are social animals and need some form of discipline in order to function effectively. They must procure food, protect their home base and their young and reproduce to keep their species going. If there were no discipline in the lives of social animals, they would eventually die from starvation and/or predation by other stronger animals.

In the case of domestic canines, discipline in their lives is needed in order for them to understand how their pack (you and other family members) functions and how they must act in order to survive.

A large humane society in a highly populated area recently surveyed dog owners regarding their satisfaction with their relationships with their dogs. People who had trained their dogs were 75% more satisfied with their pets than those who had never trained their dogs.

Dr. Edward Thorndike, a noted psychologist, established *Thorndike's Theory of Learning*, which states that a behavior that results in a pleasant event tends to be repeated. Likewise, a behavior that results in an unpleasant event tends not to be repeated. It is this theory upon which training methods are based

TRAINING RULES
If you want to be successful in
training your dog, you have four basic
rules to obey yourself:
1. Develop an understanding of how a
   dog thinks.
2. Do not blame the dog for lack of
   communication.
3. Define your dog's personality and
   act accordingly.
4. Have patience and be consistent.

today. For example, if you
manipulate a dog to perform a
specific behavior and reward him
for doing it, he is likely to do it
again because he enjoyed the end
result.

Occasionally, punishment, a
penalty inflicted for an offense, is
necessary. The best type of
punishment often comes from an
outside source. For example, a
child is told not to touch the oven
because he may get burned. He
disobeys and touches the oven. In
doing so, he receives a burn. From
that time on, he respects the heat
of the oven and avoids contact
with it. Therefore, a behavior that
results in an unpleasant event
tends not to be repeated.

A good example of a dog
learning the hard way is the dog
who chases the house cat. He is
told many times to leave the cat
alone, yet he persists in teasing
the cat. Then, one day, the dog
begins chasing the cat but the cat

turns and swipes a claw across
the dog's face, leaving the dog
with a painful gash on his nose.
The final result is that the dog
stops chasing the cat. Again, a
behavior that results in an
unpleasant event tends not to be
repeated.

TRAINING EQUIPMENT

COLLAR AND LEAD
For an Anatolian, the collar and
lead that you use for training must
be one with which you are easily
able to work, not too heavy for the
pup and perfectly safe.

TREATS
Have a bag of treats on hand;
something nutritious and easy to
swallow works best. Use a soft
treat, a chunk of cheese or a piece
of cooked chicken rather than a
dry biscuit. By the time the dog
has finished chewing a dry treat,
he will forget why he is being
rewarded in the first place!

THE GOLDEN RULE
The golden rule of dog training is
simple. For each "question"
(command), there is only one correct
answer (reaction). One command =
one reaction. Keep practicing the
command until the dog reacts
correctly without hesitating. Be
repetitive but not monotonous. Dogs
get bored just as people do!

Using food rewards will not teach a dog to beg at the table—the only way to teach a dog to beg at the table is to give him food from the table. In training, rewarding the dog with a food treat will help him associate praise and the treats with learning new behaviors that obviously please his owner.

TRAINING BEGINS: ASK THE DOG A QUESTION

In order to teach your dog anything, you must first get his attention. After all, he cannot learn anything if he is looking away from you with his mind on something else.

To get your dog's attention, ask him "School?" and immediately walk over to him and give him a treat as you tell him "Good dog." Wait a minute or two and repeat the routine, this time with a treat in your hand as you approach within a foot of the dog. Do not go directly to him, but stop about a foot short of him and hold out the treat as you ask "School?" He will see you approaching with a treat in your hand and most likely begin walking toward you. As you meet, give him the treat and praise again.

The third time, ask the question, have a treat in your hand and walk only a short distance toward the dog so that he must walk almost all the way to you. As he reaches you, give him

the treat and praise again.

By this time, the dog will probably be getting the idea that if he pays attention to you, especially when you ask that question, it will pay off in treats and enjoyable activities for him. In other words, he learns that "school" means

Your Anatolian must be taught to behave politely on-lead. A dog this large could surely take his owner for a walk!

doing great things with you that are fun and that result in positive attention for him.

Remember that the dog does not understand your verbal language; he only recognizes sounds. Your question translates to a series of sounds for him, and those sounds become the signal to go to you and pay attention. The dog learns that if he does this, he will get to interact with you plus receive treats and praise.

THE BASIC COMMANDS

TEACHING SIT

Now that you have the dog's attention, attach his lead and hold it in your left hand, and hold a food treat in your right hand. Place your food hand at the dog's nose and let him lick the treat but not take it from you. Say "Sit" and slowly raise your food hand from in front of the dog's nose up over his head so that he is looking at the ceiling. As he bends his head upward, he will have to bend his knees to maintain his balance. As he bends his knees, he will assume a sit position. At that point, release the food treat and praise lavishly with comments such as "Good dog! Good sit!" Remember to always praise enthusiastically, because dogs relish verbal praise from their owners and feel so proud of themselves whenever they accomplish a behavior.

You will not use food forever in getting the dog to obey your commands. Food is only used to teach new behaviors and, once the dog knows what you want when you give a specific command, you will wean him off the food treats but still maintain the verbal praise. After all, you will always have your voice with you, and there will be many times when you have no food rewards but expect the dog to obey.

TEACHING DOWN

Teaching the down exercise is easy when you understand how the dog perceives the down position, but it is very difficult when you do not. Dogs perceive the down position as a submissive one; therefore, teaching the down exercise by using a forceful method can sometimes make the dog develop such a fear of the down that he either runs away when you say "Down" or he attempts to snap at the person who tries to force him down.

Have the dog sit close alongside your left leg, facing in the same direction as you are. Hold the lead in your left hand and a food treat in your right. Now place your left hand lightly on the top of the dog's shoulders where they meet above the spinal cord. Do not push down on the dog's shoulders; simply rest your left hand there so you can guide the dog to lie down close to your

Teaching your dog to sit on command is a basic and necessary exercise. This young student is practicing on his own!

DOUBLE JEOPARDY

A dog in jeopardy never lies down. He stays alert on his feet because instinct tells him that he may have to run away or fight for his survival. Therefore, if a dog feels threatened or anxious, he will not lie down. Consequently, it is important to keep the dog calm and relaxed as he learns the down exercise.

When the dog's elbows touch the floor, release the food and praise softly. Try to get the dog to maintain that down position for several seconds before you let him sit up again. The goal here is to get the dog to settle down and not feel threatened in the down position.

TEACHING STAY

It is easy to teach the dog to stay in either a sit or a down position. Again, we use food and praise during the teaching process as we help the dog to understand exactly what it is that we are expecting him to do.

To teach the sit/stay, start with the dog sitting on your left side as before and hold the lead in your left hand. Have a food treat in your right hand and place your food hand at the dog's nose. Say "Stay" and step out on your right foot to stand directly in front of the dog, toe to toe, as he licks and nibbles the treat. Be sure to keep his head facing upward to maintain the sit position. Count to five and then swing around to stand next to the dog again with him on your left. As soon as you get back to the original position, release the food and praise lavishly.

left leg rather than to swing away from your side when he drops.

Now place the food hand at the dog's nose, say "Down" very softly (almost a whisper) and slowly lower the food hand to the dog's front feet. When the food hand reaches the floor, begin moving it forward along the floor in front of the dog. Keep talking softly to the dog, saying things like, "Do you want this treat? You can do this, good dog." Your reassuring tone of voice will help calm the dog as he tries to follow the food hand in order to get the treat.

To teach the down/stay, do the down as previously described. As soon as the dog lies down, say "Stay" and step out on your right foot just as you did in the sit/stay.

CONSISTENCY PAYS OFF

Dogs need consistency in their feeding schedule, exercise and relief visits, and in the verbal commands you use. If you use "Stay" on Monday and "Stay here, please" on Tuesday, you will confuse your dog. Don't demand perfect behavior during training sessions and then let him have the run of the house the rest of the day. Above all, lavish praise on your pet consistently every time he does something right. The more he feels he is pleasing you, the more willing he will be to learn.

Count to five and then return to stand beside the dog with him on your left side. Release the treat and praise as always.

Within a week or ten days, you can begin to add a bit of distance between you and your dog when you leave him. When you do, use your left hand open with the palm facing the dog as a stay signal. Hold the food treat in your right hand as before, but this time the food will not be touching the dog's nose. He will watch the food hand and quickly learn that he is going to get that treat as soon as you return to his side.

When you can stand 1 yard away from your dog for 30 seconds, you can then begin building time and distance in both stays. Eventually, the dog can be expected to remain in the stay position for prolonged periods of time until you return to him or call him to you. Always praise lavishly when he stays.

TEACHING COME

If you make teaching "come" an exciting experience, you should never have a student that does not love the game or that fails to come when called. The secret, it seems, is never to teach the word "come."

At times when an owner most wants his dog to come when called, the owner is likely to be upset or anxious and he allows these feelings to come through in

Teaching a reliable recall ("come" command) means that your Anatolian will come running whenever you call him to you.

the tone of his voice when he calls his dog. Hearing that desperation in his owner's voice, the dog fears the results of going to him and therefore either disobeys outright or runs in the opposite direction. The secret, therefore, is to teach the dog a game and, when you want him to come to you, simply play the game. It is practically a no-fail solution!

To begin, have several members of your family take a few

"COME" . . . BACK

Never call your dog to come to you for a correction or scold him when he reaches you. That is the quickest way to turn a come command into "Go away fast!" Dogs think only in the present tense, and your dog will connect the scolding with coming to you, not with the misbehavior of a few moments earlier.

"WHERE ARE YOU?"

When calling the dog, do not say "Come." Say things like, "Rover, where are you? See if you can find me! I have a biscuit for you!" Keep up a constant line of chatter with coaxing sounds and frequent questions such as, "Where are you?" The dog will learn to follow the sound of your voice to locate you and receive his reward.

food treats and each go into a different room in the house. Everyone takes turns calling the dog, and each person should celebrate the dog's finding him with a treat and lots of happy praise. When a person calls the dog, he is actually inviting the dog to find him and to get a treat as a reward for winning.

A few turns of the "Where are you?" game and the dog will understand that everyone is playing the game and that each person has a big celebration awaiting the dog's success at locating him or her. Once the dog learns to love the game, simply calling out "Where are you?" will bring him running from wherever he is when he hears that all-important question.

The come command is recognized as one of the most important things to teach a dog, but there are trainers who work with thousands of dogs and never teach the actual word "come." Yet these dogs will race to respond to a person who uses the dog's name followed by "Where are you?" For example, a woman has an elderly companion dog who went blind, but who never fails to locate her owner when asked, "Where are you?"

Children, in particular, love to play this game with their dogs. Children can hide in smaller places like a shower or bathtub, behind a bed or under a table. The dog needs to work a little bit harder to find these hiding places, but, when he does, he loves to celebrate with a treat and a tussle with a favorite youngster.

TEACHING HEEL

Heeling means that the dog walks beside the owner without pulling. It takes time and patience on the owner's part to succeed at teaching the dog that he (the owner) will not proceed unless the dog is walking calmly beside him. Neither pulling out ahead on the lead nor lagging behind is acceptable.

Begin by holding the lead in your left hand as the dog sits beside your left leg. Move the loop end of the lead to your right hand, but keep your left hand short on the lead so that it keeps the dog in close next to you.

Say "Heel" and step forward on your left foot. Keep the dog close to you and take three steps. Stop and have the dog sit next to

you in what we now call the heel position. Praise verbally, but do not touch the dog. Hesitate a moment and begin again with "Heel," taking three steps and stopping, at which point the dog is told to sit again.

Your goal here is to have the dog walk those three steps without pulling on the lead. Once he will walk calmly beside you for three steps without pulling, increase the number of steps you take to five. When he will walk politely beside you while you take five steps, you can increase the length of your walk to ten steps. Keep increasing the length of your stroll until the dog will walk quietly beside you without pulling as long as you want him to heel. When you stop heeling, indicate to the dog that the exercise is over by verbally praising as you pet him and say, "OK, good dog." The "OK" is used as a release word, meaning

Walks around the neighborhood or anywhere in public always should be on-lead to keep your dog safe and prevent him from running off after something that catches his attention.

TUG OF WALK?

If you begin teaching the heel by taking long walks and letting the dog pull you along, he misinterprets this action as an acceptable form of taking a walk. When you pull back on the lead to counteract his pulling, he reads that tug as a signal to pull even harder!

From practicing the heel exercise in the backyard... that the exercise is finished and the dog is free to relax.

If you are dealing with a dog who insists on pulling you around, simply "put on your brakes" and stand your ground until the dog realizes that the two of you are not going anywhere until he is beside you and moving at your pace, not his. It may take some time just standing there to convince the dog that you are the leader and that you will be the one to decide on the direction and speed of your travel.

Each time the dog looks up at you or slows down to give a slack lead between the two of you,

quietly praise him and say, "Good heel. Good dog." Eventually, the dog will begin to respond and within a few days he will be walking politely beside you without pulling on the lead. At first, the training sessions should be kept short and very positive; soon the dog will be able to walk nicely with you for increasingly longer distances. Remember also to give the dog free time and the opportunity to run and play when you have finished heel practice.

WEANING OFF FOOD IN TRAINING

Food is used in training new behaviors. Once the dog understands what behavior goes with a specific command, it is time to start weaning him off the food treats. At first, give a treat after each exercise. Then, start to give a treat only after every other exercise. Mix up the times when you offer a food reward and the times when you only offer praise so that the dog will never know when he is going to receive both food and praise and when he is going to receive only praise. This is called a variable ratio reward system. It proves successful because there is always the chance that the owner will produce a treat, so the dog never stops trying for that reward. No matter what, *always* give verbal praise.

OBEDIENCE CLASSES

It is a good idea to enroll in an obedience class if one is available in your area. If yours is

HEELING WELL

Teach your dog to heel in an enclosed area. Once you think the dog will obey reliably and you want to attempt advanced obedience exercises such as off-lead heeling, test him in a fenced-in area so he cannot run away.

OBEDIENCE SCHOOL

A basic obedience beginner's class usually lasts for six to eight weeks. Dog and owner attend an hour-long lesson once a week and practice for a few minutes, several times a day, each day at home. If done properly, the whole procedure will result in a well-mannered dog and an owner who delights in living with a pet that is eager to please and enjoys doing things with his owner.

a show dog, handling classes would be more appropriate. Many areas have dog clubs that offer basic obedience training as well as preparatory classes for obedience competition. There are also local dog trainers who offer similar classes.

At obedience trials, dogs can earn titles at various levels of competition. The beginning levels of obedience competition include basic behaviors such as sit, down, heel, etc. The more advanced levels of competition include jumping, retrieving, scent discrimination and signal work.

...to heeling on-lead beautifully in the show ring.

While obedience trials are popular with many breeds, it is not a sport in which Anatolians usually participate.

OTHER ACTIVITIES FOR LIFE

Whether a dog is trained in the structured environment of a class or alone with his owner at home, there are many activities that can bring fun and rewards to both owner and dog once they have mastered basic control.

Teaching the dog to help out around the home, in the yard or on the farm provides great satisfaction to both dog and owner. In addition, the dog's help makes life a little easier for his owner and raises his stature as a valued companion to his family. It helps give the dog a purpose by occupying his mind and providing an outlet for his energy.

Backpacking is an exciting and healthy activity that the dog can be taught without assistance from more than his owner. The exercise of walking and climbing is good for man and dog alike, and the bond that they develop together is priceless. The rule for backpacking with any dog is never to expect the dog to carry more than one-sixth of his body weight.

If you are interested in participating in organized competition with your Anatolian, there are activities other than obedience in which you and your dog can become involved. Agility is a popular sport in which dogs run through an obstacle course that includes various jumps, tunnels and other exercises to test the dog's speed and coordination. The owners run beside their dogs to give commands and to guide them through the course. Although competitive, the focus is on fun— it's fun to do, fun to watch and great exercise.

STUDENT'S STRESS TEST

During training sessions, you must be able to recognize signs of stress in your dog such as:
- tucking his tail between his legs
- lowering his head
- shivering or trembling
- standing completely still or running away
- panting and/or salivating
- avoiding eye contact
- flattening his ears back
- urinating submissively
- rolling over and lifting a leg
- grinning or baring teeth
- aggression when restrained

If your four-legged student displays these signs, he may just be nervous or intimidated. The training session may have been too lengthy, with not enough praise and affirmation. Stop for the day and try again tomorrow.

This youngster looks very pleased with learning his lessons, and his owner must be equally delighted.

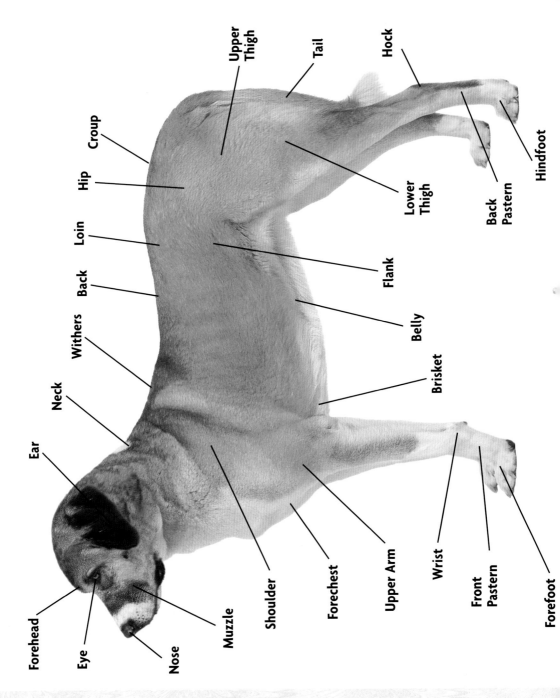

PHYSICAL STRUCTURE OF THE ANATOLIAN SHEPHERD DOG

HEALTH CARE OF YOUR
ANATOLIAN SHEPHERD DOG

Dogs suffer from many of the same physical illnesses as people and might even share many of the same psychological problems. Since people usually know more about human diseases than canine maladies, many of the terms used in this chapter will be familiar but not necessarily those used by vets. For example, we will use the familiar term *x-ray* instead of *radiograph*. We will also use the familiar term *symptoms*, even though dogs don't have symptoms, which are verbal descriptions of something the patient feels or observes himself that he regards as abnormal. Dogs have *clinical signs* since they cannot speak, so we have to look for these clinical signs...but we still use the term *symptoms* in this book.

Medicine is a constantly changing art, with some scientific input as well. Things alter as we learn more and more about basic sciences such as genetics and biochemistry, and have use of more sophisticated imaging techniques like Computer Aided Tomography (CAT scans) or Magnetic Resonance Imaging (MRI scans). There is academic dispute about many canine maladies, so different vets treat them in different ways, and some vets have a greater emphasis on surgical techniques than others.

SELECTING A QUALIFIED VET
Your selection of a vet should be based on personal recommendation for his skills and experience with large-breed dogs. If the vet is based nearby, it will be helpful because you might have an emergency or need to make multiple visits for treatments.

All veterinary professionals are licensed and are capable of handling routine medical issues such as infections, injuries and the promotion of health (for example, by vaccination). If the problem affecting your dog is more complex, your vet will refer your pet to someone with a more detailed knowledge of what is wrong. This could be a specialist at the nearest university veterinary school who is a veterinary dermatologist, veterinary ophthalmologist, etc; whatever is the relevant field.

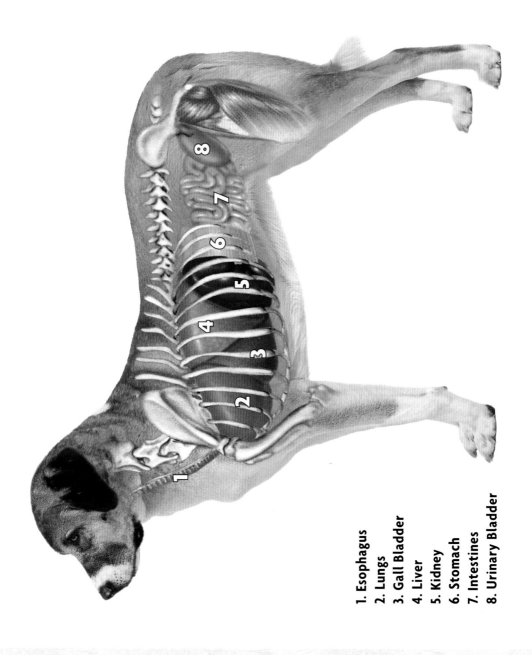

1. Esophagus
2. Lungs
3. Gall Bladder
4. Liver
5. Kidney
6. Stomach
7. Intestines
8. Urinary Bladder

INTERNAL ORGANS OF THE ANATOLIAN SHEPHERD DOG

Veterinary procedures are very costly and, as the treatments available improve, they are going to become more expensive. It is quite acceptable to discuss matters of cost with your vet; if there is more than one treatment option, cost may be a factor in deciding which route to take.

PREVENTATIVE MEDICINE

It is much easier, less costly and more effective to practice preventative medicine than to fight bouts of illness and disease. Properly bred puppies of all breeds come from parents that were selected based upon their genetic disease profiles. The puppies' mother should have been vaccinated, free of all internal and external parasites and properly nourished. For these reasons, a visit to the vet who cared for the dam is recommended if at all possible. The dam passes disease resistance to her puppies, which should last from eight to ten weeks. Unfortunately, she can also pass on parasites and infection. This is why knowledge about her health is useful in learning more about the health of the puppies.

WEANING TO FIVE MONTHS OLD

Puppies should be weaned by the time they are two months old. A puppy that remains for at least eight weeks with his dam and

Breakdown of Veterinary Income by Category

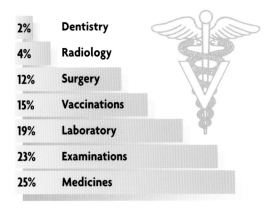

2%	Dentistry
4%	Radiology
12%	Surgery
15%	Vaccinations
19%	Laboratory
23%	Examinations
25%	Medicines

A typical vet's income, categorized according to services performed. This survey dealt with small-animal (pets) practices.

littermates usually adapts better to other dogs and people later in life.

Some new owners have their puppy examined by a vet immediately, which is a good idea unless the puppy is overtired by a long journey home from the breeder. Vaccination programs usually begin when the puppy is very young.

The puppy will have his teeth examined and have his skeletal conformation and general health checked prior to certification by the veterinarian. Puppies in certain breeds have problems with their kneecaps, cataracts and other eye problems, heart murmurs and undescended testicles. They may also have personality problems and your vet might have training in temperament evaluation.

VACCINATION SCHEDULING

Most vaccinations are given by injection and should only be

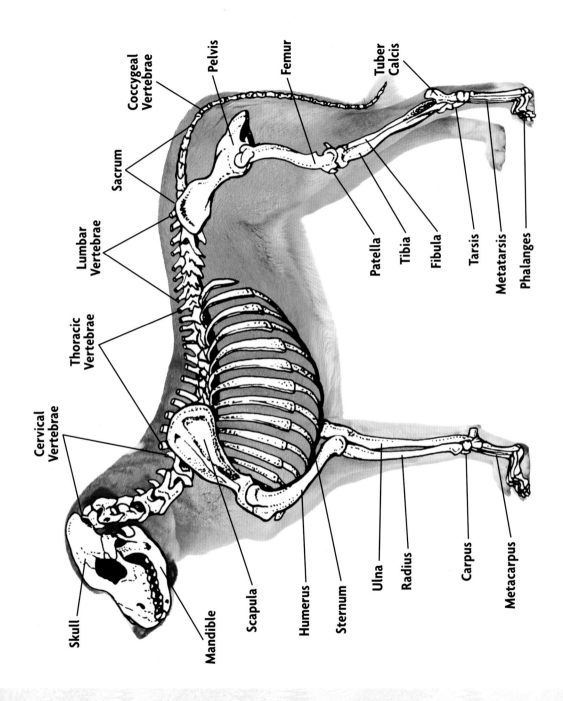

Coccygeal Vertebrae

Pelvis

Femur

Tuber Calcis

Sacrum

Patella

Tibia

Fibula

Tarsis

Metatarsis

Phalanges

Lumbar Vertebrae

Thoracic Vertebrae

Cervical Vertebrae

Skull

Mandible

Scapula

Humerus

Sternum

Ulna

Radius

Carpus

Metacarpus

SKELETAL STRUCTURE OF THE ANATOLIAN SHEPHERD DOG

MORE THAN VACCINES

Vaccinations help prevent your new puppy from contracting diseases, but they do not cure them. Proper nutrition as well as parasite control keep your dog healthy. Remember that your dog depends on you to ensure his well-being.

given by a vet. Both he and you should keep a record of the date of the injection, the identification of the vaccine and the amount given. Some vets give a first vaccination at eight weeks, but

most dog breeders prefer the course not to commence until about ten weeks because of interaction with the antibodies produced by the dam. The vaccination scheduling is usually based on a 15-day cycle. You must take your vet's advice as to when to vaccinate, as this may differ according to the vaccine used.

The usual vaccines contain immunizing doses of several different viruses such as distemper, parvovirus, parainfluenza and hepatitis. There are other vaccines available when the puppy is at risk. You should

HEALTH AND VACCINATION SCHEDULE

Age in Weeks:	6th	8th	10th	12th	14th	16th	20-24th	52nd
Worm Control	✔	✔	✔	✔	✔	✔	✔	
Neutering								✔
Heartworm		✔		✔		✔	✔	
Parvovirus	✔		✔		✔		✔	✔
Distemper		✔		✔		✔		✔
Hepatitis		✔		✔		✔		✔
Leptospirosis								✔
Parainfluenza	✔		✔		✔			✔
Dental Examination		✔					✔	✔
Complete Physical		✔					✔	✔
Coronavirus				✔			✔	✔
Kennel Cough	✔							
Hip Dysplasia								✔
Rabies							✔	

Vaccinations are not instantly effective. It takes about two weeks for the dog's immune system to develop antibodies. Most vaccinations require annual booster shots. Your veterinarian should guide you in this regard.

rely upon professional advice. This is especially true for the booster immunizations. Most vaccination programs require a booster when the puppy is a year old and once a year thereafter. In some cases, circumstances may require more or less frequent immunizations.

Kennel cough, more formally known as tracheobronchitis, is immunized against with a vaccine that is sprayed into the dog's nostrils. Kennel cough is usually included in routine vaccination, but it is often not as effective as the vaccines for other major diseases.

FIVE MONTHS TO ONE YEAR OF AGE
Unless you intend to breed or show your dog, neutering the puppy at six months of age is recommended. Discuss this with your veterinarian. Neutering/ spaying has proven to be

What's itching your dog? Sometimes a pup just needs to scratch, while other times scratching indicates a problem. Check your Anatolian's skin and coat often for any signs of parasites, irritation, rash, etc.

DISEASE REFERENCE CHART

	What is it?	What causes it?	Symptoms
Leptospirosis	Severe disease that affects the internal organs; can be spread to people.	A bacterium, which is often carried by rodents, that enters through mucous membranes and spreads quickly throughout the body.	Range from fever, vomiting and loss of appetite in less severe cases to shock, irreversible kidney damage and possibly death in most severe cases.
Rabies	Potentially deadly virus that infects warm-blooded mammals.	Bite from a carrier of the virus, mainly wild animals.	1st stage: dog exhibits change in behavior, fear. 2nd stage: dog's behavior becomes more aggressive. 3rd stage: loss of coordination, trouble with bodily functions.
Parvovirus	Highly contagious virus, potentially deadly.	Ingestion of the virus, which is usually spread through the feces of infected dogs.	Most common: severe diarrhea. Also vomiting, fatigue, lack of appetite.
Kennel cough	Contagious respiratory infection.	Combination of types of bacteria and virus. Most common: *Bordetella bronchiseptica* bacteria and parainfluenza virus.	Chronic cough.
Distemper	Disease primarily affecting respiratory and nervous system.	Virus that is related to the human measles virus.	Mild symptoms such as fever, lack of appetite and mucous secretion progress to evidence of brain damage, "hard pad."
Hepatitis	Virus primarily affecting the liver.	Canine adenovirus type I (CAV-1). Enters system when dog breathes in particles.	Lesser symptoms include listlessness, diarrhea, vomiting. More severe symptoms include "blue-eye" (clumps of virus in eye).
Coronavirus	Virus resulting in digestive problems.	Virus is spread through infected dog's feces.	Stomach upset evidenced by lack of appetite, vomiting, diarrhea.

extremely beneficial to male and female puppies, respectively. Besides eliminating the possibility of pregnancy, it inhibits (but does not prevent) breast cancer in bitches and prostate cancer in male dogs. Under no circumstances should a bitch be spayed prior to her first season.

Your vet should provide your puppy with a thorough dental evaluation at six months of age, ascertaining whether all the permanent teeth have erupted properly. A home dental-care regimen should be initiated at six months, including brushing weekly and providing good dental devices (such as nylon bones). Regular dental care promotes healthy teeth, fresh breath and a longer life.

DOGS OLDER THAN ONE YEAR
Continue to visit the vet at least once a year. There is no such disease as "old age," but bodily functions do change with age. The eyes and ears are no longer as efficient. Liver, kidney and intestinal functions often decline. Regular veterinary care and proper dietary changes, recommended by your vet, can make life more pleasant for your aging Anatolian and you.

SKIN PROBLEMS

Vets are consulted by dog owners for skin problems more than for any other group of diseases or maladies. A dog's skin is as sensitive, if not more so, than human skin, and both suffer from almost the same ailments (though the occurrence of acne in dogs is rare!). For this reason, veterinary dermatology has developed into a specialty practiced by many veterinary professionals.

Since many skin problems have visual symptoms that are almost identical, it requires the skill of an experienced veterinary dermatologist to identify and cure many of the more severe skin disorders. Pet shops sell many treatments for skin problems, but most of the treatments are directed at symptoms and not at the underlying problem(s). If your dog is suffering from a skin disorder, you should seek professional assistance as quickly as possible. As with all diseases, the earlier a problem is identified and treated, the more likely that the cure will be successful.

HEREDITARY SKIN DISORDERS

Veterinary dermatologists are currently researching a number of skin disorders that are believed to have a hereditary basis. These inherited diseases are transmitted by both parents, who appear (phenotypically) normal but have a recessive gene for the disease, meaning that they carry, but are not affected by, the disease. These diseases pose serious problems to breeders because in some instances there are no methods of identifying carriers. Often the secondary diseases associated with these skin conditions are even more debilitating than the skin disorders themselves, including cancers and respiratory problems.

Among the hereditary skin disorders for which the mode of inheritance is known are acrodermatitis, cutaneous asthenia (Ehlers-Danlos syndrome), sebaceous adenitis, cyclic hematopoiesis, dermatomyositis, IgA deficiency, color dilution alopecia and nodular dermatofibrosis. Some of these disorders are limited to one or two breeds, while others affect a large number of breeds. All inherited diseases must be diagnosed and treated by a veterinary specialist.

PARASITE BITES

Many of us are allergic to insect bites. The bites itch, erupt and may even become infected. Dogs have the same reaction to fleas, ticks and/or mites. When an insect lands on you, you have the chance to whisk it away with your hand. Unfortunately, when a dog is bitten by a flea, tick or mite, it can only scratch it away or bite it. By the time the dog has been bitten, the parasite has done some of its damage. It may also have laid eggs, which will cause further problems in the near future. The itching from parasite bites is probably due to the saliva injected into the site when the parasite sucks the dog's blood.

AIRBORNE ALLERGIES

Just as humans suffer from hay fever and other airborne allergies during the pollinating season, many dogs suffer from the same allergies. When the pollen count is high, your dog might suffer, but don't expect him to sneeze and have a runny nose like a human would. Dogs react to pollen allergies in the same way they react to fleas—they scratch and bite themselves. Dogs, like humans, can be tested for allergens. Discuss the testing with your vet.

VITAL SIGNS

A dog's normal temperature is 101.5°F (38.6°C). A range of between 100.0 and 102.5°F (37.8°–39°C) should be considered normal, as each dog's body sets its own temperature. It will be helpful if you take your dog's temperature when you know he is healthy and record it. Then, when you suspect that he is not feeling well, you will have a normal figure to compare the abnormal temperature against.

The normal pulse rate for a dog is between 100 and 125 beats per minute.

ACRAL LICK GRANULOMA

Many large dogs have a very poorly understood syndrome called acral lick granuloma. The manifestation of the problem is the dog's tireless attack at a specific area of the body, almost always the legs or paws. The dog licks so intensively that he removes the hair and skin, leaving an ugly, large wound. Tiny protuberances, which are outgrowths of new capillaries, bead on the surface of the wound. Owners who notice their dogs' biting and chewing at their extremities should have the vet determine the cause. If lick granuloma is identified, although there is no absolute cure, corticosteroids are the most common treatment.

AUTO-IMMUNE ILLNESSES

An auto-immune illness is one in which the immune system overacts and does not recognize parts of the affected person (or dog); rather, the immune system starts to react as if these parts were foreign and need to be destroyed. An example is rheumatoid arthritis, which occurs when the body does not recognize the joints, thus leading to a very painful and damaging reaction in the joints. This has nothing to do with age, so can occur in children as well as adults. The wear-and-tear arthritis of the older person or dog is osteoarthritis.

Lupus is one auto-immune disease that affects dogs as well as people. It can take variable forms, affecting the kidneys, bones and the skin. It can be fatal, so is treated with steroids, which can themselves have very significant side effects. The steroids calm down the allergic reaction to the body's tissues, which helps the lupus, but also decreases the body's reaction to real foreign substances such as bacteria, and also thins the skin and bone.

FOOD PROBLEMS

FOOD ALLERGIES

Dogs are allergic to many foods that are best-sellers and highly recommended by breeders and vets. Changing the brand of food that you buy may not eliminate the problem if the element to which the dog is allergic is contained in the new brand.

Recognizing a food allergy can be difficult. Humans often have rashes when they eat foods to which they are allergic, or have swelling of the lips or eyes. Dogs do not usually develop rashes, but react in the same way as they do to an airborne or bite allergy—they itch, scratch and bite. While pollen allergies and parasite bites are usually seasonal, pollen allergies are year-round problems.

Diagnosis of a food allergy is based on a two- to four-week dietary trial with a home-cooked diet fed to the exclusion of all other foods. The diet should consist of boiled rice or potato with a source of protein that the dog has never eaten before, such as fresh or frozen fish, lamb or even something as exotic as pheasant. Water has to be the only drink, and it is really important that no other foods are fed during this trial. If the dog's condition improves, you will need to try the original diet once again to see if the itching resumes. If it does, then this confirms the diagnosis that the dog is allergic to his original diet. The treatment is long-term feeding of something that does not distress the dog's skin, which may be in the form of one of the commercially available hypoallergenic diets or the home-made diet that you created for the allergy trial.

FOOD INTOLERANCE

Food intolerance is the inability of the dog to completely digest certain foods. This occurs because the dog does not have the chemicals necessary to digest some foodstuffs. These chemicals are called enzymes. All puppies have the enzymes necessary to digest canine milk, but some dogs do not have the enzymes to digest a very different form of

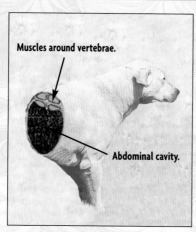

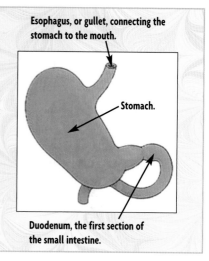

Fig. 1 (Left): Cross-section through an Anatolian Shepherd Dog. **Fig. 2 (Right):** The stomach hangs like a handbag with both straps broken within the deep body cavity. Support is provided by the junction with the esophagus and the junction with the duodenum.

Muscles around vertebrae.

Abdominal cavity.

Esophagus, or gullet, connecting the stomach to the mouth.

Stomach.

Duodenum, the first section of the small intestine.

milk that is commonly found in human households—milk from cows. In such dogs, drinking cows' milk results in loose bowels, stomach pains and the passage of gas.

Dogs often do not have the enzymes to digest soy or other beans. The treatment is to exclude the foodstuffs that upset your Anatolian's digestion.

BLOAT OR GASTRIC TORSION
This is the greatest killer of large, deep-chested breeds, and is the subject of much research, but still manages to take away many dogs before their time and in a very horrible way.

The diagram showing a cross-section through an Anatolian (Fig. 1) shows how deep the body cavity is. The muscles shown are those around the vertebrae that give strength to the back and allow it to be flexed and stretched when running. The stomach hangs like a handbag with both straps broken within this deep body cavity. (Fig. 2)

The second cross-section (Fig. 3) is similar, but it demonstrates another way in which the stomach is held in place. There is support provided by the junction with the esophagus or gullet, and there is support provided by the junction with the first part of the small intestine, the "broken straps of the handbag." The only other support is a thin layer of partially opaque "internal skin" called the peritoneum.

It is no wonder that the stomach can move around easily. Those breeds with the deepest chests are at the greatest risk of having their whole stomachs twist around (gastric torsion). This cuts off the blood supply and prevents the stomach's contents from leaving, and increases the amount of gas in the stomach. Once these things have happened, surgery is vital. If the blood supply has been cut off too long and a bit of the stomach wall dies, death of the Anatolian is almost inevitable.

The horrendous pain of this condition is due to the stomach wall's being stretched by the gas caught in the stomach, as well as the stomach wall's desperately needing the blood that cannot get to it. There is the pain of not being able to pass a much greater than normal amount of wind; added to this is a pain equivalent to that of a heart attack, which is due to the heart muscle's being starved of blood.

HOW TO PREVENT BLOAT

Here are some tips on how to reduce the risk of bloat in your Anatolian:

- Do not exercise your Anatolian immediately before feeding (wait at least an hour);
- Do not exercise your Anatolian immediately after feeding (wait at least an hour);
- Do not feed cheap food with high cereal content;
- Feed high-quality, low-residue diets;
- Elevate food and water bowls to try to reduce any air swallowed;
- If your Anatolian is greedy and eats quickly, reduce the air swallowed by putting something large and inedible in the food bowl so that the dog has to pick around the object and thus eat more slowly.

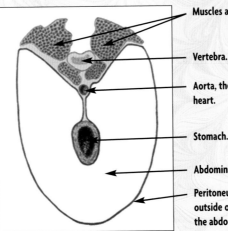

Fig. 3: Aside from the support provided by the junction with the esophagus and the support provided by the junction with the first part of the small intestine, the only other support is from a thin layer of "internal skin" called the peritoneum.

Muscles around the vertebra.

Vertebra.

Aorta, the main blood vessel from the heart.

Stomach.

Abdominal cavity.

Peritoneum, the thin membrane lining the outside of the stomach and the inside of the abdominal cavity.

DETECTING BLOAT

The following are symptoms of bloat and require immediate veterinary attention:

- Your dog's stomach starts to distend, ending up large and as tight as a football;
- Your dog is dribbling, as no saliva can be swallowed;
- Your dog makes frequent attempts to vomit but cannot bring anything up due to the stomach's being closed off;
- Your dog is distressed from pain;
- Your dog starts to suffer from clinical shock, meaning that there is not enough blood in the dog's circulation as the hard, dilated stomach stops the blood from returning to the heart to be pumped around the body. Clinical shock is indicated by pale gums and tongue, as they have been starved of blood. The shocked dog also has glazed, staring eyes.

You have minutes, yes, *minutes*, to get your dog into surgery. If you see any of these symptoms at any time of the day or night, get to the vet immediately, as that is where all the equipment is located. Someone will have to phone and warn that you are on your way (which is a justification for the invention of the cellular phone!), so that they can be prepared to get your pet on the operating

A SKUNKY PROBLEM

Have you noticed your dog dragging his rump along the floor? If so, it is likely that his anal sacs are impacted or possibly infected. The anal sacs are small pouches located on both sides of the anus under the skin and muscles. They are about the size and shape of a grape and contain a foul-smelling liquid. Their contents are usually emptied when the dog has a bowel movement but, if not emptied completely, they will impact, which will cause your dog much pain. Fortunately, your veterinarian can tend to this problem easily by draining the sacs for the dog. Be aware that your dog might also empty his anal sacs in cases of extreme fright.

table. Always remember, with any surgical procedure, to remind the veterinarian and technicians about the Anatolian's sensitivity to anesthesia.

It is possible for a dog to have more than one incident of gastric torsion, even if it has had his stomach stapled, in which the stomach is stapled to the inside of the chest wall to give extra support and prevent its twisting again.

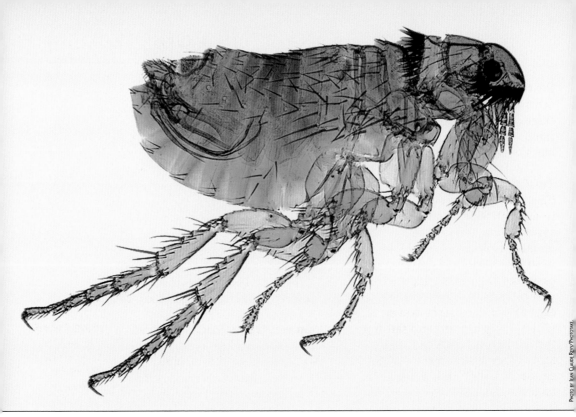

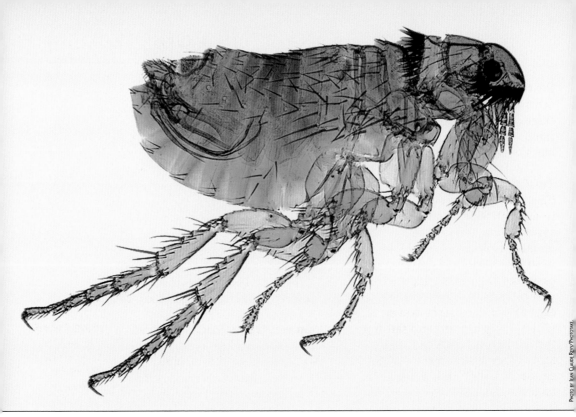

Photo by Jean Claude Revy/Phototake.

A male dog flea,
*Ctenocephalides
canis.*

EXTERNAL PARASITES

FLEAS

Of all the problems to which dogs are prone, none is more well known and frustrating than fleas. Flea infestation is relatively simple to cure but difficult to prevent. Parasites that are harbored inside the body are a bit more difficult to eradicate but they are easier to control.

To control flea infestation, you have to understand the flea's life cycle. Fleas are often thought of as a summertime problem, but centrally heated homes have changed the patterns and fleas can be found at any time of the year.

The most effective method of flea control is a two-stage approach: one stage to kill the adult fleas, and the other to control the development of pre-adult fleas. Unfortunately, no single active ingredient is effective against all stages of the life cycle.

LIFE CYCLE STAGES

During its life, a flea will pass through four life stages: egg, larva, pupa or nymph and adult. The adult stage is the most visible and irritating stage of the flea life cycle, and this is why the majority of flea-control products concentrate on this stage. The fact is that adult fleas account for only 1% of the total flea population, and the other 99% exist in pre-adult stages, i.e., eggs, larvae and pupae. The pre-adult stages are barely visible to the naked eye.

THE LIFE CYCLE OF THE FLEA

Eggs are laid on the dog, usually in quantities of about 20 or 30, several times a day. The adult female flea must have a blood meal before each egg-laying session. When first laid, the eggs will cling to the dog's hair, as the eggs are still moist. However, they will quickly dry out and fall from the dog, especially if the dog moves around or scratches. Many eggs will fall off in the dog's favorite area or an area in which he spends a lot of time, such as his bed.

Once the eggs fall from the dog onto the carpet or furniture, they will hatch into larvae. This takes from one to ten days. Larvae are not particularly mobile and will usually travel only a few inches

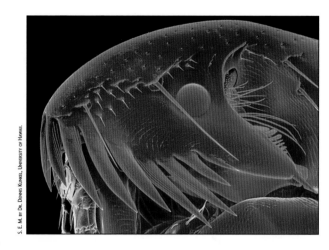

S. E. M. BY DR. DENNIS KUNKEL, UNIVERSITY OF HAWAII.

from where they hatch. However, they do have a tendency to move away from heavy traffic and light—under furniture and behind doors are common places to find high quantities of flea larvae.

The flea larvae feed on dead organic matter, including adult flea feces, until they are ready to change into adult fleas. Fleas will usually remain as larvae for around seven days. After this period, the larvae will pupate into protective pupae or nymphs. While inside the pupae, the larvae will undergo metamorphosis and change into adult fleas. This can take as little time as a few days, but the adult fleas can remain inside the pupae waiting to hatch for up to two years. The pupae are signaled to hatch by certain stimuli, such as physical pressure—the pupae's being stepped on, heat from an animal's lying on the pupae or increased

Magnified head of a dog flea, *Ctenocephalides canis*, colorized for effect.

FLEA KILLER CAUTION— "POISON"

Flea killers are poisonous. You should not spray these toxic chemicals on areas of a dog's body that he licks, including his genitals and his face. Flea killers taken internally are a better answer, but check with your vet in case internal therapy is not advised for your dog.

The dog flea is the most common parasite found on pet dogs.

S. E. M. BY DR. DENNIS KUNKEL, UNIVERSITY OF HAWAII.

carbon-dioxide levels and vibrations—indicating that a suitable host is available.

Once hatched, the adult flea must feed within a few days. Once the adult flea finds a host, it will not leave voluntarily. It only becomes dislodged by grooming or the host animal's scratching. The adult flea will remain on the host for the duration of its life unless forcibly removed.

Dwight R. Kuhn's magnificent action photo, showing a flea jumping from a dog's back.

PHOTO BY DWIGHT R. KUHN.

TREATING THE ENVIRONMENT AND THE DOG

Treating fleas should be a two-pronged attack. First, the environment needs to be treated; this includes carpets and furniture, especially the dog's bedding and areas underneath furniture. The environment should be treated with a household spray containing an Insect Growth Regulator (IGR) and an insecticide to kill the adult fleas. Most IGRs are effective against eggs and larvae; they actually mimic the fleas' own hormones and stop the eggs and larvae from developing into adult fleas. There are currently no treatments available to attack the pupa stage of the life cycle, so the adult insecticide is used to kill the newly hatched adult fleas before they find a host. Most IGRs are active for many months, while adult insecticides are only active for a few days.

When treating with a household spray, it is a good idea to vacuum before applying the product. This stimulates as many pupae as possible to hatch into adult fleas. The vacuum cleaner should also be treated with an insecticide to prevent the eggs and larvae that have been collected in the vacuum bag from hatching.

The second stage of treatment is to apply an adult insecticide to the dog.

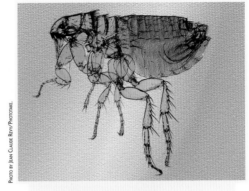

EN GARDE: CATCHING FLEAS OFF GUARD!

Consider the following ways to arm yourself against fleas:

- Add a small amount of pennyroyal or eucalyptus oil to your dog's bath. These natural remedies repel fleas.
- Supplement your dog's food with fresh garlic (minced or grated) and a hearty amount of brewer's yeast, both of which ward off fleas.
- Use a flea comb on your dog daily. Submerge fleas in a cup of bleach to kill them quickly.
- Confine the dog to only a few rooms to limit the spread of fleas in the home.
- Vacuum daily...and get all of the crevices! Dispose of the bag every few days until the problem is under control.
- Wash your dog's bedding daily. Cover cushions where your dog sleeps with towels, and wash the towels often.

A LOOK AT FLEAS

Fleas have been around for millions of years and have adapted to changing host animals. They are able to go through a complete life cycle in less than one month or they can extend their lives to almost two years by remaining as pupae or cocoons. They do not need blood or any other food for up to 20 months.

They have been measured as being able to jump 300,000 times and can jump 150 times their length in any direction, including straight up. Those are just a few of the reasons why they are so successful in infesting a dog!

THE LIFE CYCLE OF THE FLEA

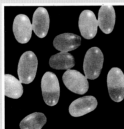

Egg

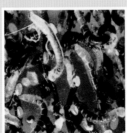

Larva

Pupa or Nymph

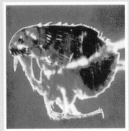

Adult

A scanning electron micrograph of a dog or cat flea, *Ctenocephalides*, magnified more than 100x. This image has been colorized for effect.

Traditionally, this would be in the form of a collar or a spray, but more recent innovations include digestible insecticides that poison the fleas when they ingest the dog's blood. Alternatively, there are drops that, when placed on the back of the dog's neck, spread throughout the hair and skin to kill adult fleas.

INSECT GROWTH REGULATOR (IGR)

Two types of products should be used when treating fleas—a product to treat the pet and a product to treat the home. Adult fleas represent less than 1% of the flea population. The pre-adult fleas (eggs, larvae and pupae) represent more than 99% of the flea population and are found in the environment; it is in the case of pre-adult fleas that products containing an Insect Growth Regulator (IGR) should be used in the home.

IGRs are a modern class of compounds used to prevent the development of insects. They do not kill the insect outright, but instead use the insect's biology against it to stop it from completing its growth. Products that contain methoprene are the world's first and leading IGRs. Used to control fleas and other insects, this type of IGR will stop flea larvae from developing and protect the house for up to seven months.

DO NOT MIX

Never mix flea-control products without first consulting your vet. Some products can become toxic when combined with others and can cause fatal consequences.

TICKS AND MITES

Though not as common as fleas, ticks and mites are found all over the tropical and temperate world. They don't bite, like fleas; they harpoon. They dig their sharp proboscis (nose) into the dog's skin and drink the blood. Their only food and drink is dog's blood. Dogs can get Lyme disease, Rocky Mountain spotted fever, tick bite paralysis and many other diseases from ticks and mites. They may live where fleas are found and they like to hide in cracks or seams in walls. They are controlled the same way fleas are controlled.

The American dog tick, *Dermacentor variabilis*, may well be the most common dog tick in many geographical areas, especially those areas where the climate is hot and humid. Most

A brown dog tick, *Rhipicephalus sanguineus*, is an uncommon but annoying tick found on dogs.

PHOTO BY CAROLINA BIOLOGICAL SUPPLY/PHOTOTAKE.

The head of an American dog tick, *Dermacentor variabilis*, enlarged and colorized for effect.

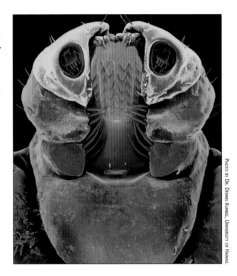

Photo by Dr. Dennis Kunkel, University of Hawaii.

The great outdoors may be fun for your dog, but it also is a home to dangerous ticks. Deer ticks carry a bacterium known as *Borrelia burgdorferi* and are most active in the autumn and spring. When infections are caught early, penicillin and tetracycline are effective antibiotics, but if left untreated the bacteria may cause neurological, kidney and cardiac problems as well as long-term trouble with walking and painful joints.

S. E. M. by Dr. Andrew Spielman/Phototake.

dog ticks have life expectancies of a week to six months, depending upon climatic conditions. They can neither jump nor fly, but they can crawl slowly and can range up to 6 feet to reach a sleeping or unsuspecting dog.

Human lice look like dog lice; the two are closely related.

Photo by Dwight R. Kuhn.

Mange

Mites cause a skin irritation called mange. Some mites are contagious, like *Cheyletiella*, ear mites, scabies and chiggers. Mites that infest ears are usually controlled with ivermectin, which can only be administered by a vet in most states, followed by Tresaderm at home. It is essential that your dog be treated for mange as quickly as possible because some forms of mange are transmissible to people.

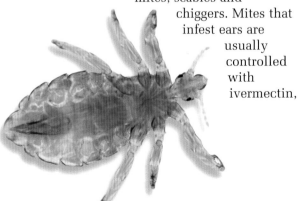

Opposite page:
The American dog tick, *Dermacentor variabilis*, is probably the most common tick found on dogs. Look at the strength in its eight legs! No wonder it's hard to detach them.

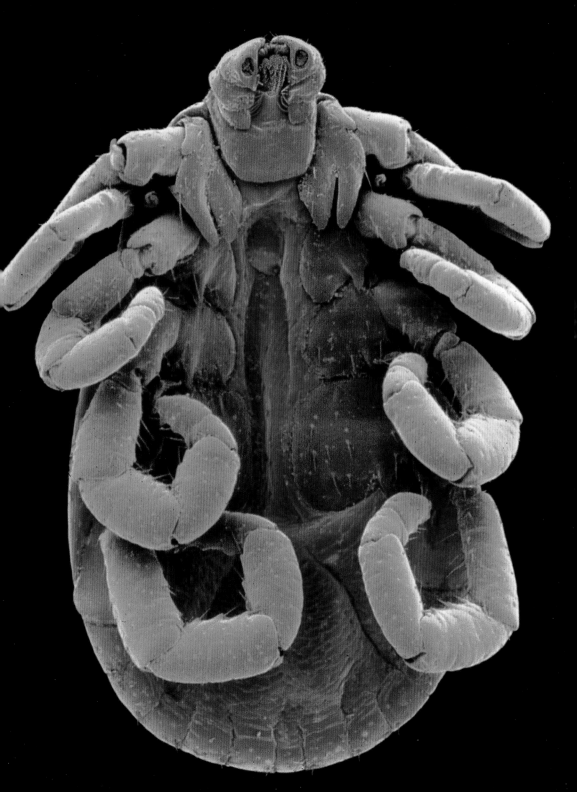

The mange mite,
Psoroptes bovis.

INTERNAL PARASITES

Most animals—fishes, birds and mammals, including dogs and humans—have worms and other parasites that live inside their bodies. According to Dr. Herbert R. Axelrod, the fish pathologist, there are two kinds of parasites: dumb and smart. The smart parasites live in peaceful cooperation with their hosts (symbiosis), while the dumb parasites kill their hosts. Most worm infections are relatively easy to control. If they are not controlled, they weaken the host dog to the point that other medical problems occur, but they do not kill the host as dumb parasites would.

ROUNDWORMS

The roundworms that infect dogs are known scientifically as *Toxocara canis*. They live in the dog's intestines and shed eggs continually. It has been estimated that a dog produces about 6 or more ounces of feces every day. Each ounce of feces averages hundreds of thousands of roundworm eggs. There are no known areas in which dogs roam that do not contain roundworm eggs. The greatest danger of

ROUNDWORMS

Average-size dogs can pass 1,360,000 roundworm eggs every day. For example, if there were only 1 million dogs in the world, the world would be saturated with thousands of tons of dog feces. These feces would contain around 15 billion round-worm eggs.

Up to 31% of home yards and children's sand boxes contain roundworm eggs.

Flushing dog's feces down the toilet is not a safe practice because the usual sewage treatments do not destroy roundworm eggs.

Infected puppies start shedding roundworm eggs at three weeks of age. They can be infected by their mother's milk.

PHOTO BY CAROLINA BIOLOGICAL SUPPLY/PHOTOTAKE.

The roundworm *Rhabditis* can infect both dogs and humans.

roundworms is that they infect people too! It is wise to have your dog tested regularly for roundworms.

Pigs also have roundworm infections that can be passed to humans and dogs. The typical roundworm parasite is called *Ascaris lumbricoides.*

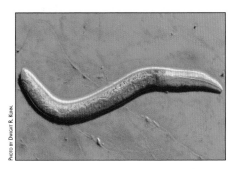

PHOTO BY DWIGHT R. KUHN.

DEWORMING

Ridding your puppy of worms is *very important* because certain worms that puppies carry, such as tapeworms and roundworms, can infect humans.

Breeders initiate deworming programs at or about four weeks of age. The routine is repeated every two or three weeks until the puppy is three months old. The breeder from whom you obtained your puppy should provide you with the complete details of the deworming program.

Your veterinarian can prescribe and monitor the program of deworming for you. The usual program is treating the puppy every 15–20 days until the puppy is positively worm-free. It is advised that you only treat your puppy with drugs that are recommended professionally.

The common roundworm, *Ascaris lumbricoides.*

Left: The hookworm *Ancylostoma caninum.*

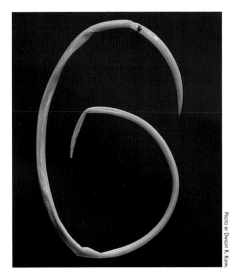

PHOTO BY DWIGHT R. KUHN.

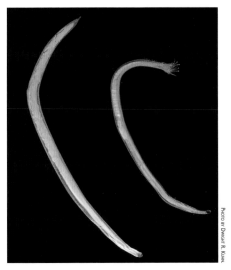

PHOTO BY DWIGHT R. KUHN.

Right: Male and female hookworms.

HOOKWORMS

The worm *Ancylostoma caninum* is commonly called the dog hookworm. It is also dangerous to humans and cats. It has teeth by which it attaches itself to the intestines of the dog. It changes the site of its attachment about six times a day and the dog loses blood from each detachment, possibly causing iron-deficiency anemia. Hookworms are easily purged from the dog with many medications. Milbemycin oxime, which also serves as a heartworm preventative in Collies, can be

The infective stage of the hookworm larva.

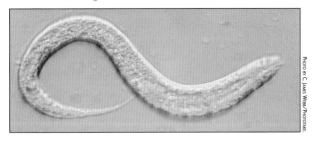

PHOTO BY C. JAMES WEBB/PHOTOTAKE.

used for this purpose.

In some regions, the "temperate climate" hookworm (*Uncinaria stenocephala*) is rarely found in pet or show dogs, but can occur in hunting packs, racing Greyhounds and sheepdogs because the worms can be prevalent wherever dogs are exercised regularly on grassland.

TAPEWORMS

There are many species of tapeworm, all of which are carried by fleas! The dog eats the flea and starts the tapeworm cycle. Humans can also be infected with tapeworms—so don't eat fleas! Fleas are so small that your dog could pass them onto your hands, your plate or your food, and thus make it possible for you to ingest a flea that is carrying tapeworm eggs.

TAPEWORMS

Humans, rats, squirrels, foxes, coyotes, wolves and domestic dogs are all susceptible to tapeworm infection. Except in humans, tapeworms are usually not a fatal infection. Infected individuals can harbor 1000 parasitic worms.

Tapeworms, like some other types of worm, are hermaphroditic, meaning male and female in the same worm.

If dogs eat infected rats or mice, they get the tapeworm disease. One month after attaching to a dog's intestine, the worm starts shedding eggs. These eggs are infective immediately. Infective eggs can live for a few months without a host animal.

While tapeworm infection is not life-threatening in dogs (smart parasite!), it can be the cause of a very serious liver disease for humans. About 50% of the humans infected with *Echino-coccus multilocularis*, a type of tapeworm that causes alveolar hydatis, perish.

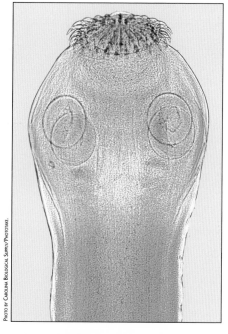

The head and rostellum (the round prominence on the scolex) of a tapeworm, which infects dogs and humans.

PHOTO BY CAROLINA BIOLOGICAL SUPPLY/PHOTOTAKE.

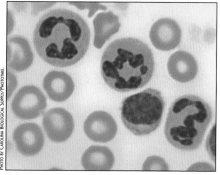

Magnified heartworm larvae, *Dirofilaria immitis*.

PHOTO BY CAROLINA BIOLOGICAL SUPPLY/PHOTOTAKE.

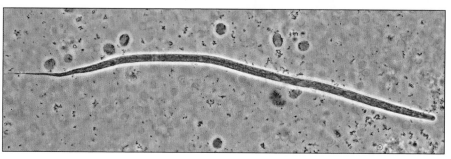

Heartworm, *Dirofilaria immitis*.

PHOTO BY J E HAYDEN, RBP/PHOTOTAKE.

A vet with experience in large-breed dogs will be better equipped to handle the specific problems and requirements of your Anatolian Shepherd.

HEARTWORMS

Heartworms are thin, extended worms up to 12 inches (30.4 cms) long, which live in a dog's heart and the major blood vessels surrounding it. Dogs may have up to 200 worms. Symptoms may be loss of energy, loss of appetite, coughing, the development of a pot belly and anemia.

Heartworms are transmitted by mosquitoes. The mosquito drinks the blood of an infected dog and takes in larvae with the blood. The larvae, called microfilariae, develop within the body of the mosquito and are passed on to the next dog bitten after the larvae mature. It takes two to three weeks for the larvae to develop to the infective stage within the body of the mosquito. Dogs are usually treated at about six weeks of age, and maintained on a prophylactic dose given monthly.

Blood testing for heartworms is not necessarily indicative of how seriously your dog is infected. This is a dangerous disease. Discuss the various preventatives with your vet, as some are not recommended for herding dogs. Together you can choose a safe course of prevention for your Anatolian Shepherd.

The heart of a dog infected with canine heartworm, *Dirofilaria immitis.*

HOMEOPATHY:
an alternative
to conventional
medicine

"Less Is Most"
Using this principle, the strength
of a homeopathic remedy is
measured by the number of
serial dilutions that were
undertaken to create it. The
greater the number of serial
dilutions, the greater the
strength of the homeopathic
remedy. The potency of a
remedy that has been made by
making a dilution of 1 part in
100 parts (or 1/100) is 1c or 1cH.
If this remedy is subjected to a
series of further dilutions, each
one being 1/100, a more dilute
and stronger remedy is
produced. If the remedy is
diluted in this way six times, it is
called 6c or 6cH. A dilution of 6c
is 1 part in 1,000,000,000,000. In
general, higher potencies in
more frequent doses are better
for acute symptoms and lower
potencies in more infrequent
doses are more useful for
chronic, long-standing problems.

CURING OUR DOGS NATURALLY
Holistic medicine means treating the whole animal as a unique, perfect living being. Generally, holistic treatments do not suppress the symptoms that the body naturally produces, as do most medications prescribed by conventional doctors and vets. Holistic methods seek to cure disease by regaining balance and harmony in the patient's environment. Some of these methods include use of nutritional therapy, herbs, flower essences, aromatherapy, acupuncture, massage, chiropractic and, of course, the most popular holistic approach, homeopathy.

Homeopathy is a theory or system of treating illness with small doses of substances which, if administered in larger quantities, would produce the symptoms that the patient already has. This approach is often described as "like cures like." Although modern veterinary medicine is geared toward the "quick fix," homeopathy relies on the belief that, given the time, the body is able to heal itself and return to its natural, healthy state.

Choosing a remedy to cure a problem in our dogs is the difficult part of homeopathy. Consult with your vet for a professional diagnosis of your dog's symptoms. Often these symptoms require immediate conventional care. If your vet is willing, and knowledgeable, you may attempt a homeopathic remedy. Be aware that cortisone prevents homeopathic remedies from working. There are hundreds of possibilities and combinations to cure many problems in dogs, from basic physical problems such as excessive shedding, fleas or other parasites, unattractive doggy odor, bad breath, upset tummy, obesity, dry, oily or dull coat, diarrhea, ear problems or eye discharge (including tears and dry or mucousy matter), to behavioral abnormalities such as fear of loud noises, habitual licking, poor appetite, excessive barking and various phobias. From alumina to zincum metallicum, the remedies span the planet and the imagination…from flowers and weeds to chemicals, insect droppings, diesel smoke and volcanic ash.

Using "Like to Treat Like"

Unlike conventional medicines that suppress symptoms, homeopathic remedies treat illnesses with small doses of substances that, if administered in larger quantities, would produce the symptoms that the patient already has. While the same homeopathic remedy can be used to treat different symptoms in different dogs, here are some interesting remedies and their uses.

Apis Mellifica
(made from honey bee venom) can be used for allergies or to reduce swelling that occurs in acutely infected kidneys.

Diesel Smoke
can be used to help control motion sickness.

Calcarea Fluorica
(made from calcium fluoride, which helps harden bone structure) can be useful in treating hard lumps in tissues.

Natrum Muriaticum
(made from common salt, sodium chloride) is useful in treating thin, thirsty dogs.

Nitricum Acidum
(made from nitric acid) is used for symptoms you would expect to see from contact with acids, such as lesions, especially where the skin joins the linings of body orifices or openings such as the lips and nostrils.

Symphytum
(made from the herb Knitbone, *Symphytum officianale*) is used to encourage bones to heal.

Urtica Urens
(made from the common stinging nettle) is used in treating painful, irritating rashes.

HOMEOPATHIC REMEDIES FOR YOUR DOG

Symptom/Ailment	Possible Remedy
ALLERGIES	Apis Mellifica 30c, Astacus Fluviatilis 6c, Pulsatilla 30c, Urtica Urens 6c
ALOPECIA	Alumina 30c, Lycopodium 30c, Sepia 30c, Thallium 6c
ANAL GLANDS (BLOCKED)	Hepar Sulphuris Calcareum 30c, Sanicula 6c, Silicea 6c
ARTHRITIS	Rhus Toxicodendron 6c, Bryonia Alba 6c
CATARACT	Calcarea Carbonica 6c, Conium Maculatum 6c, Phosphorus 30c, Silicea 30c
CONSTIPATION	Alumina 6c, Carbo Vegetabilis 30c, Graphites 6c, Nitricum Acidum 30c, Silicea 6c
COUGHING	Aconitum Napellus 6c, Belladonna 30c, Hyoscyamus Niger 30c, Phosphorus 30c
DIARRHEA	Arsenicum Album 30c, Aconitum Napellus 6c, Chamomilla 30c, Mercurius Corrosivus 30c
DRY EYE	Zincum Metallicum 30c
EAR PROBLEMS	Aconitum Napellus 30c, Belladonna 30c, Hepar Sulphuris 30c, Tellurium 30c, Psorinum 200c
EYE PROBLEMS	Borax 6c, Aconitum Napellus 30c, Graphites 6c, Staphysagria 6c, Thuja Occidentalis 30c
GLAUCOMA	Aconitum Napellus 30c, Apis Mellifica 6c, Phosphorus 30c
HEAT STROKE	Belladonna 30c, Gelsemium Sempervirens 30c, Sulphur 30c
HICCOUGHS	Cinchona Deficinalis 6c
HIP DYSPLASIA	Colocynthis 6c, Rhus Toxicodendron 6c, Bryonia Alba 6c
INCONTINENCE	Argentum Nitricum 6c, Causticum 30c, Conium Maculatum 30c, Pulsatilla 30c, Sepia 30c
INSECT BITES	Apis Mellifica 30c, Cantharis 30c, Hypericum Perforatum 6c, Urtica Urens 30c
ITCHING	Alumina 30c, Arsenicum Album 30c, Carbo Vegetabilis 30c, Hypericum Perforatum 6c, Mezerium 6c, Sulphur 30c
KENNEL COUGH	Drosera 6c, Ipecacuanha 30c
MASTITIS	Apis Mellifica 30c, Belladonna 30c, Urtica Urens 1m
MOTION SICKNESS	Cocculus 6c, Petroleum 6c
PATELLAR LUXATION	Gelsemium Sempervirens 6c, Rhus Toxicodendron 6c
PENIS PROBLEMS	Aconitum Napellus 30c, Hepar Sulphuris Calcareum 30c, Pulsatilla 30c, Thuja Occidentalis 6c
PUPPY TEETHING	Calcarea Carbonica 6c, Chamomilla 6c, Phytolacca 6c

Recognizing a Sick Dog

Unlike colicky babies and cranky children, our canine charges cannot tell us when they are feeling ill. Therefore, there are a number of signs that owners can identify to know that their dogs are not feeling well.

Take note for physical manifestations such as:

- unusual, bad odor, including bad breath
- excessive shedding
- wax in the ears, chronic ear irritation
- oily, flaky, dull haircoat
- mucus, tearing or similar discharge in the eyes
- fleas or mites
- mucus in stool, diarrhea
- sensitivity to petting or handling
- licking at paws, scratching face, etc.

Keep an eye out for behavioral changes as well including:

- lethargy, idleness
- lack of patience or general irritability
- lack of appetite
- phobias (fear of people, loud noises, etc.)
- strange behavior, suspicion, fear
- coprophagia
- more frequent barking
- whimpering, crying

Get Well Soon

You don't need a DVM to provide good TLC to your sick or recovering dog, but you do need to pay attention to some details that normally wouldn't bother him. The following tips will aid Fido's recovery and get him back on his paws again:

- Keep his space free of irritating smells, like heavy perfumes and air fresheners.
- Rest is the best medicine! Avoid harsh lighting that will prevent your dog from sleeping. Shade him from bright sunlight during the day and dim the lights in the evening.
- Keep the noise level down. Animals are more sensitive to sound when they are sick.

- Be attentive to any necessary temperature adjustments. A dog with a fever needs a cool room and cold liquids. A bitch that is whelping or recovering from surgery will be more comfortable in a warm room, consuming warm liquids and food.
- You wouldn't send a sick child back to school early, so don't rush your dog back into a full routine until he seems absolutely ready.

Number-One Killer Disease in Dogs: CANCER

In every age, there is a word associated with a disease or plague that causes humans to shudder. In the 21st century, that word is "cancer." Just as cancer is the leading cause of death in humans, it claims nearly half the lives of dogs that die from a natural disease as well as half the dogs that die over the age of ten years.

Described as a genetic disease, cancer becomes a greater risk as the dog ages. Vets and dog owners have become increasingly aware of the threat of cancer to dogs. Statistics reveal that one dog in every five will develop cancer, the most common of which is skin cancer. Many cancers, including prostate, ovarian and breast cancer, can be avoided by spaying and neutering our dogs by the age of six months.

Early detection of cancer can save or extend a dog's life, so it is absolutely vital for owners to have their dogs examined by a qualified vet or oncologist immediately upon detection of any abnormality. Certain dietary guidelines have also proven to reduce the onset and spread of cancer. Foods based on fish rather than beef, due to the presence of Omega-3 fatty acids, are recommended. Other amino acids such as glutamine have significant benefits for canines, particularly those breeds that show a greater susceptibility to cancer.

Cancer management and treatments promise hope for future generations of canines. Since the disease is genetic, breeders should never breed a dog whose parents, grandparents and any related siblings have developed cancer. It is difficult to know whether to exclude an otherwise healthy dog from a breeding program as the disease does not manifest itself until the dog's senior years.

RECOGNIZE CANCER WARNING SIGNS

Since early detection can possibly rescue your dog from becoming a cancer statistic, it is essential for owners to recognize the possible signs and seek the assistance of a qualified professional.

- Abnormal bumps or lumps that continue to grow
- Bleeding or discharge from any body cavity
- Persistent stiffness or lameness
- Recurrent sores or sores that do not heal
- Inappetence
- Breathing difficulties
- Weight loss
- Bad breath or odors
- General malaise and fatigue
- Eating and swallowing problems
- Difficulty urinating and defecating

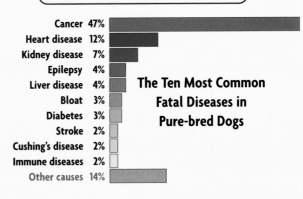

Disease	%
Cancer	47%
Heart disease	12%
Kidney disease	7%
Epilepsy	4%
Liver disease	4%
Bloat	3%
Diabetes	3%
Stroke	2%
Cushing's disease	2%
Immune diseases	2%
Other causes	14%

The Ten Most Common Fatal Diseases in Pure-bred Dogs

First Aid at a Glance

Burns
Place the affected area under cool water; use ice if only a small area is burnt.

Insect bites
Apply ice to relieve swelling; antihistamine dosed properly.

Animal bites
Clean any bleeding area; apply pressure until bleeding subsides; go to the vet.

Spider bites
Use cold compress and a pressurized pack to inhibit venom's spreading.

Antifreeze poisoning
Induce vomiting with hydrogen peroxide. Seek *immediate* veterinary help!

Fish hooks
Removal best handled by vet; hook must be cut in order to remove.

Snake bites
Pack ice around bite; contact vet quickly; identify snake for proper antivenin.

Car accident
Move dog from roadway with blanket; seek veterinary aid.

Shock
Calm the dog; keep him warm; seek immediate veterinary help.

Nosebleed
Apply cold compress to the nose; apply pressure to any visible abrasion.

Bleeding
Apply pressure above the area; treat wound by applying a cotton pack.

Heat stroke
Submerge dog in cold bath; cool down with fresh air and water; go to the vet.

Frostbite/Hypothermia
Warm the dog with a warm bath, electric blankets or hot water bottles.

Abrasions
Clean the wound and wash out thoroughly with fresh water; apply antiseptic.

 Remember: an injured dog may attempt to bite a helping hand from fear and confusion. Always muzzle the dog before trying to offer assistance.

A naturally hardy breed, the Anatolian Shepherd Dog enjoys a long lifespan with proper everyday care and regular veterinary checkups.

CDS: COGNITIVE DYSFUNCTION SYNDROME
"OLD-DOG SYNDROME"

There are many ways to evaluate old-dog syndrome. Vets have defined CDS (cognitive dysfunction syndrome) as the gradual deterioration of cognitive abilities. These are indicated by changes in the dog's behavior. When a dog changes his routine response, and maladies have been eliminated as the cause of these behavioral changes, then CDS is the usual diagnosis.

More than half the dogs over eight years old suffer from some form of CDS. The older the dog, the more chance it has of suffering from CDS. In humans, doctors often dismiss the CDS behavioral changes as part of "winding down."

There are four major signs of CDS: frequent potty accidents inside the home, sleeping much more or much less than normal, acting confused and failure to respond to social stimuli.

SYMPTOMS OF CDS

FREQUENT POTTY ACCIDENTS
- *Urinates in the house.*
- *Defecates in the house.*
- *Doesn't signal that he wants to go out.*

SLEEP PATTERNS
- *Moves much more slowly.*
- *Sleeps more than normal during the day.*
- *Sleeps less during the night.*

CONFUSION
- *Goes outside and just stands there.*
- *Appears confused with a faraway look in his eyes.*
- *Hides more often.*
- *Doesn't recognize friends.*
- *Doesn't come when called.*
- *Walks around listlessly and without a destination.*

FAILURE TO RESPOND TO SOCIAL STIMULI
- *Comes to people less frequently, whether called or not.*
- *Doesn't tolerate petting for more than a short time.*
- *Doesn't come to the door when you return home.*

ANATOLIAN SHEPHERD DOG

The term "old" is a qualitative term. For dogs, as well as for their masters, old is relative. Certainly we can all distinguish between a puppy Anatolian and an adult Anatolian—there are the obvious physical traits, such as size, appearance and facial expressions, as well as personality traits. Puppies and young dogs like to play with children. Children's natural exuberance is a good match for the seemingly endless energy of young dogs. They like to run, jump, chase and retrieve. When dogs grow older and cease their interaction with children, they are often thought of as being too old to keep pace with the kids. On the other hand, if an Anatolian is only exposed to older people or quieter lifestyles, his life will normally be less active and the decrease in his activity level as he ages will not be as obvious.

If people live to be 100 years old, dogs live to be 20 years old. While this might seem like a good rule of thumb, it is very inaccurate. When trying to compare dog years to human years, you cannot make a generalization about all dogs. While most large-breed dogs do not last until 10 years of age, the Anatolian commonly lives to be 12 to 14 years of age.

Dogs generally are considered physically mature at three years of age (or earlier), but can reproduce even earlier. The Anatolian is not considered physically mature, in some cases, until four years of age. Generally speaking, the first three years of a dog's life are like seven times that of comparable humans. That means a 3-year-old dog is like a 21-year-old human. As the curve of comparison shows, there is no hard and fast rule for comparing dog and human ages. Small breeds tend to live longer than large breeds, some breeds' adolescent periods last longer than others' and some breeds experience rapid periods of growth. The comparison is made even more difficult, for, likewise, not all humans age at the same rate...and human females live longer than human males.

WHAT TO LOOK FOR IN SENIORS

Most vets and behaviorists use the seven-year mark as the time to consider a dog a "senior" or "veteran," though some breeders prefer to wait until the Anatolian is eight or nine years of age. Nevertheless, the term "senior" does not imply that the dog is geriatric and has begun to fail in mind and body. Aging is essentially a slowing process. Humans readily admit that they feel a difference in their activity level from age 20 to 30, and then from 30 to 40, etc. By treating the seven-year-old dog as a senior, owners are able to implement certain therapeutic and preventative medical strategies with the help of their vets.

A senior-care program should include at least two veterinary visits per year and screening sessions to determine the dog's health status, as well as nutritional counseling. Vets determine the senior dog's health status through a blood smear for a complete blood count, serum chemistry profile with electrolytes, urinalysis, blood pressure check, electrocardiogram, ocular tonometry (pressure on the eyeball) and dental prophylaxis.

Such an extensive program for senior dogs is well advised before owners start to see the obvious physical signs of aging, such as slower and inhibited movement, graying, increased sleep/nap periods and disinterest in play and other activity. This preventative program promises a longer, healthier life for the aging dog. Among the physical problems

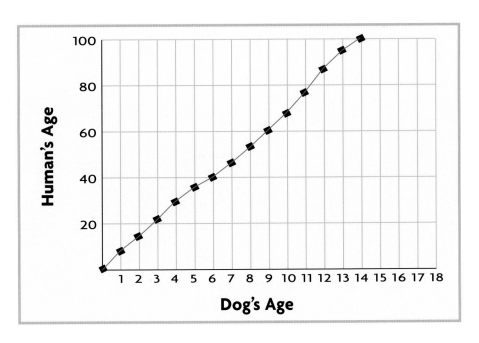

common in aging dogs are the loss of sight and hearing, arthritis, kidney and liver failure, diabetes mellitus, heart disease and Cushing's disease (a hormonal disease).

In addition to the physical manifestations discussed, there are some behavioral changes and problems related to aging dogs. Dogs suffering from hearing or vision loss, dental discomfort or arthritis can become aggressive. Likewise, the near-deaf and/or blind dog may be startled more easily and react in an unexpectedly aggressive manner. Seniors suffering from senility can become more impatient and irritable. Housesoiling accidents are associated with loss of mobility, kidney problems and loss of sphincter control as well as plaque accumulation, physiological brain changes and reactions to medications. Older dogs, just like young puppies, suffer from separation anxiety, which can lead to excessive barking, whining, housesoiling and destructive behavior. Seniors may become fearful of everyday sounds, such as vacuum cleaners, heaters, thunder and passing traffic. Some dogs have difficulty sleeping, due to discomfort, the need for frequent relief and the like.

Owners should avoid spoiling the older dog with too many fatty treats. Obesity is a common problem in older dogs and

subtracts years from their lives. Keep the senior dog as trim as possible, since excessive weight puts additional stress on the body's vital organs. Some breeders recommend supplementing the diet with foods high in fiber and lower in calories. Adding fresh vegetables and marrow broth to the senior's diet makes a tasty, low-calorie, low-fat supplement. Vets also offer specialty diets for senior dogs that are worth exploring.

Your dog, as he nears his

NOTICING THE SYMPTOMS

The symptoms listed below are symptoms that gradually appear and become more noticeable. They are not life-threatening; however, these symptoms are to be taken very seriously and warrant a discussion with your vet:

• Your dog cries and whimpers when he moves, and he stops running completely.

• Convulsions start or become more serious and frequent. The usual convulsion (spasm) is when the dog stiffens and starts to tremble, being unable or unwilling to move. The seizure usually lasts for 5 to 30 minutes.

• Your dog drinks more water and urinates more frequently. Wetting and bowel accidents take place indoors without warning.

• Vomiting becomes more and more frequent.

twilight years, needs your patience and good care more than ever. Never punish an older dog for an accident or abnormal behavior. For all the years of love, protection and companionship that your dog has provided, he deserves special attention and courtesies. The older dog may need to relieve himself at 3 a.m. because he can no longer hold it for eight hours. Older dogs may not be able to remain crated for more than two or three hours. It may be time to give up a sofa or chair to your old friend. Although he may not seem as enthusiastic about your attention and petting, he does appreciate the considerations you offer as he gets older.

Your Anatolian does not understand why his world is slowing down. Owners must make their dogs' transition into their golden years as pleasant and rewarding as possible.

WHAT TO DO WHEN THE TIME COMES

You are never fully prepared to make a rational decision about putting your dog to sleep. It is very obvious that you love your Anatolian or you would not be reading this book. Putting a beloved dog to sleep is extremely difficult. It is a decision that must be made with your vet. You are usually forced to make the decision when your dog experiences one or more life-threatening symptoms that have become serious enough for you to seek veterinary help.

If the prognosis of the malady indicates that the end is near and that your beloved pet will only continue to suffer and experience no enjoyment for the balance of his life, then euthanasia is the right choice.

WHAT IS EUTHANASIA?
Euthanasia derives from the Greek, meaning "good death." In other words, it means the planned, painless killing of a dog suffering from a painful, incurable condition, or who is so aged that he cannot walk, see, eat or control his excretory functions. Euthanasia is usually accomplished by injection with an overdose of anesthesia or a barbiturate. Aside from the prick of the needle, the experience is usually painless.

MAKING THE DECISION
The decision to euthanize your dog is never easy. The days during which the dog becomes ill and the end occurs can be unusually stressful for you. If this is your first experience with the death of a loved one, you may need the comfort dictated by your religious beliefs. If you are the head of the family and have children, you should have involved them in the decision of putting your Anatolian to sleep. Usually your dog can be maintained on drugs for a few

Many cities have pet cemeteries located nearby. Your vet can help you locate one if you choose this option.

days in order to give you ample time to make a decision. During this time, talking with members of your family or with people who have lived through the same experience can ease the burden of your inevitable decision.

THE FINAL RESTING PLACE

Dogs can have some of the same privileges as humans. The remains of your beloved dog can be buried in a pet cemetery, which is generally expensive. Dogs who have died at home can be buried on your property in a place suitably marked with some stone or newly planted tree or bush, in places where this is allowed. Alternatively, your dog can be cremated individually and the ashes returned to you. A less expensive option is mass cremation, although, of course,

TO THE RESCUE

Some people choose to adopt or "rescue" an older dog instead of buying a new puppy. Some older dogs may have come from abusive environments and be fearful, while other dogs may have developed many bad habits; both situations can present challenges to their new owners. Training an older dog will take more time and patience, but persistence and an abundance of praise and love can transform a dog into a well-behaved, loyal companion.

the ashes then cannot be returned. Vets can usually arrange the cremation on your behalf. The cost of these options should always be discussed frankly and openly with your vet.

GETTING ANOTHER DOG?

The grief of losing your beloved dog will be as lasting as the grief of losing a human friend or relative. In most cases, if your dog died of old age (if there is such a thing), it had slowed down considerably. Do you want a new Anatolian puppy to replace it? Or are you better off finding a more mature Anatolian, say two to three years of age, which will usually be house-trained and will have an already developed personality. In this case, you can find out if you like each other after a few hours of being together.

Some pet cemeteries have facilities to store urns that contain dogs' ashes after cremation.

The decision is, of course, your own. Do you want another Anatolian or perhaps a different breed so as to avoid comparison with your beloved friend? Most people usually buy the same breed because they know (and love) the characteristics of that breed. Then, too, they often know people who have the same breed and perhaps they are lucky enough that a breeder they know and respect expects a litter soon. What could be better?

A grave marker and flowers memorialize a beloved canine friend.

SHOWING YOUR
ANATOLIAN SHEPHERD DOG

When you purchase your Anatolian, you will make it clear to the breeder whether you want one just as a lovable companion and pet, or if you hope to be buying an Anatolian with show prospects. No reputable breeder will sell you a young puppy and tell you that it is *definitely* of show quality, for so much can go wrong during the early months of a puppy's development. If you plan to show, what you will hopefully have acquired is a puppy with "show potential."

To the novice, exhibiting an Anatolian in the show ring may look easy, but it takes an excellent dog and a lot of hard work and devotion to do top winning at shows such as the prestigious Westminster Kennel Club, Crufts or World Dog Show, not to mention a little luck too!

The first concept that the canine novice learns when watching a dog show is that each dog first competes against members of his own breed. Once the judge has selected the best member of each breed (Best of

CANINE GOOD CITIZEN® PROGRAM

Have you ever considered getting your dog "certified"? The AKC's Canine Good Citizen® Program affords your dog just that opportunity. Your dog shows that he is a well-behaved canine citizen, using the basic training and good manners you have taught him, by taking a series of ten tests that illustrate that he can behave properly at home, in a public place and around other dogs. The tests are administered by participating dog clubs, colleges, 4-H clubs, scouts and other community groups and are open to all pure-bred and mixed-breed dogs. Upon passing the ten tests, the suffix CGC is then applied to your dog's name.

The ten tests are: 1. Accepting a friendly stranger; 2. Sitting politely for petting; 3. Appearance and grooming; 4. Walking on a lead; 5. Walking through a group of people; 6. Sit, down and stay on command; 7. Coming when called; 8. Meeting another dog; 9. Calm reaction to distractions; 10. Separation from owner.

TEMPERAMENT PLUS
Although it seems that physical conformation is the only factor considered in the show ring, temperament is also of utmost importance. An aggressive or fearful dog should not be shown, as bad behavior will not be tolerated and may pose a threat to the judge, other exhibitors, you and your dog.

Breed), provided that the show is judged on a Group system, that chosen dog will compete with other dogs in its group. Finally, the dogs chosen first in each group will compete for Best in Show.

The second concept that you must understand is that the dogs are not actually compared against one another. The judge compares each dog against its breed standard. While some early breed standards were indeed based on specific dogs that were famous or popular, many dedicated enthusiasts say that a perfect specimen, as described in the standard, has never walked into a show ring, has never been bred and, to the woe of dog breeders around the globe, does not exist. Breeders attempt to get as close to this ideal as possible with every litter, but theoretically the "perfect" dog is so elusive that it is impossible. (And if the "perfect" dog were born, breeders and judges would never agree that it was indeed "perfect.")

If you are interested in exploring the world of dog

A line of Anatolians is stacked in the ring, as the judge considers each dog and decides which one is closest to the ideal set forth in the breed standard.

showing, your best bet is to join your local breed club or the national parent club. These clubs often host both regional and national specialties, shows only for Anatolians, which can include conformation as well as various trials. Even if you have no intention of competing with your Anatolian, a specialty is a like a festival for lovers of the breed who congregate to share their favorite topic: Anatolian Shepherd Dogs! Clubs also send out newsletters, and some

organize training days and seminars in order that people may learn more about their chosen breed. To locate the breed club closest to you, contact the national kennel club (in the US, the American Kennel Club; in Britain, The Kennel Club, etc.), which furnishes the rules and regulations for all of these events plus general dog registration and other basic requirements of dog ownership.

If your Anatolian is of age and registered, you can enter him in a dog show where the breed is offered classes. Only unaltered dogs can be entered in a dog show, so if you have spayed or neutered your Anatolian, you cannot compete in conformation shows. The reason for this is simple. Dog shows are the main forum to prove which representatives in a breed are worthy of being bred. Only dogs that have achieved championships—the recognized "seal of approval" for quality in pure-bred dogs—should be bred. Altered dogs, however, can participate in other events such as obedience trials and the Canine Good Citizen® program.

Before you actually step into the ring, you would be well advised to sit back and observe the judge's ring procedure. If it is your first time in the ring, do not be over-anxious and run to the front of the line. It is much better

Bait is a helpful tool in the show ring to get the dog to stand at attention and look his best.

INFORMATION ON CLUBS

You can get information about dog shows from the national kennel clubs:

American Kennel Club
5580 Centerview Dr., Raleigh, NC 27606-3390
USA
www.akc.org

Canadian Kennel Club
89 Skyway Ave., Suite 100, Etobicoke,
Ontario M9W 6R4 Canada
www.ckc.ca

Fédération Cynologique Internationale
14, rue Leopold II, B-6530 Thuin, Belgium
www.fci.be

The Kennel Club
1-5 Clarges St., Piccadilly,
London W1Y 8AB, UK
www.the-kennel-club.org.uk

always listen since some judges change their directions—and the judge is always right!). Finally, the judge will give the dog one last look before moving on to the next exhibitor.

If you are not in the top four in your class at your first show, do not be discouraged. Be patient and consistent, and you may eventually find yourself in a

FIVE CLASSES AT SHOWS

At most AKC all-breed shows, there are five regular classes offered: Puppy, Novice, Bred-by-Exhibitor, American-bred and Open. The Puppy Class is usually divided as 6 to 9 months of age and 9 to 12 months of age. When deciding in which class to enter your dog, male or female, you must carefully check the show schedule to make sure that you have selected the right class. Depending on the age of the dog, his previous first-place wins and the sex of the dog, you must make the best choice. It is possible to enter a one-year-old dog who has not won sufficient first places in any of the non-Puppy Classes, though the competition is more intense the further you progress from the Puppy Class.

to stand back and study how the exhibitor in front of you is performing.

The judge asks each handler to "stack" the dog, hopefully showing the dog off to his best advantage. The judge will observe the dog from a distance and from different angles, and approach the dog to check his teeth, overall structure, alertness and muscle tone, as well as consider how well the dog "conforms" to the standard. Most importantly, the judge will have the exhibitor gait the dog around the ring in some pattern that he should specify (another advantage to not going first, but

winning line-up. Remember that the winners were once in your shoes and have devoted many hours and much money to earn the placement. If you find that your dog is losing every time and never getting a nod, it may be time to consider a different dog sport or to just enjoy your Anatolian as a pet. Parent clubs offer other events, such as obedience, agility, tracking, instinct tests and more, which may be of interest to the owner of a well-trained Anatolian.

AGILITY TRIALS

Having had its origins in the UK back in 1977, agility had its

SHOW QUALITY SHOWS

While you may purchase a puppy in the hope of having a successful career in the show ring, it is impossible to tell, at eight to ten weeks of age, whether your dog will be a contender. Some promising pups end up with minor to serious faults that prevent them from taking home awards, but this certainly does not mean they can't be the best of companions for their families. To find out if your potential show dog is show-quality, enter him in a match to see how a judge evaluates him. You may also take him back to your breeder as he matures to see what the breeder might advise.

official beginning in the AKC in August 1994, when the first licensed agility trials were held. The AKC allows all registered breeds (including Miscellaneous Class breeds) to participate, providing the dog is 12 months of age or older. Agility is designed so that the handler demonstrates how well the dog can work at his side. The handler directs his dog over an obstacle course that includes different types of jumps as well as tires, the dog walk, weave poles, pipe tunnels, collapsed tunnels, etc. While working his way through the course, the dog must keep one eye and ear on the handler and the rest of his body on the course. The handler gives verbal and hand signals to guide the dog through the course.

The first organization to promote agility trials in the US was the United States Dog Agility Association, Inc. (USDAA), which was established in 1986 and spawned numerous member clubs around the country. Both the USDAA and the AKC offer titles to winning dogs. Three titles are available through the USDAA: Agility Dog (AD), Advanced Agility Dog (AAD) and Master Agility Dog (MAD). The AKC offers Novice

Congratulations! A successful outing for dog and handler as the day's winner has been selected.

Agility (NA), Open Agility (OA), Agility Excellent (AX) and Master Agility Excellent (MX). Beyond these four AKC titles, dogs can win additional ones in "jumper" classes, Jumpers with Weave Novice (NAJ), Open (OAJ) and Excellent (MXJ), which lead to the ultimate title(s): MACH, Master Agility Champion. Dogs can continue to add number designations to the MACH titles, indicating how many times the dog has met the MACH require-ments, such as MACH1, MACH2, and so on.

Agility is great fun for dog and owner with many rewards for everyone involved. Interested owners should join a training club that has obstacles and experienced agility handlers who can introduce you and your dog to the "ropes" (and tires, tunnels, jumps, etc.).

TRACKING

Any dog is capable of tracking, using his nose to follow a trail. Tracking tests are exciting and competitive ways to test your Anatolian's ability to search and

> **NEATNESS COUNTS**
> Surely you've spent hours preparing your dog for the show ring, but don't forget about yourself! While the dog should be the center of attention, it is important that you also appear neat and clean. Wear smart, appropriate clothes and comfortable shoes in a color that contrasts with your dog's coat. Look and act like a professional.

rescue. The AKC started tracking tests in 1937, when the first AKC-licensed test took place as part of the Utility level at an obedience trial. Ten years later in 1947, the AKC offered the first title, Tracking Dog (TD). It was not until 1980 that the AKC added the Tracking Dog Excellent title (TDX), which was followed by the Versatile Surface Tracking title (VST) in 1995. The title Champion Tracker (CT) is awarded to a dog who has earned all three titles.

In the beginning level of tracking, the owner follows the dog through a field on a long

> **NO SHOW**
> Never show a dog that is sick or recovering from surgery or infection. Not only will this put your own dog under a tremendous amount of stress but you will also put other dogs at risk of contracting any illness your dog has. Likewise, bitches who are in heat will distract and disrupt the performances of males who are competing, and bitches who are pregnant will likely be stressed and exhausted by a long day of showing.

PRACTICE AT HOME

If you have decided to show your dog, you must train him to gait around the ring by your side at the correct pace and pattern, and to tolerate being handled and examined by the judge. Most breeds require complete dentition, all breeds require a particular bite (scissors, level or undershot) and all males must have two apparently normal testicles fully descended into the scrotum. Enlist family and friends to hold mock trials in your yard to prepare your future champion!

lead. To earn the TD title, the dog must follow a track laid by a human 30 to 120 minutes prior. The track is about 500 yards with up to five directional changes. The TDX requires that the dog follow a track that is three to five hours old over a course up to 1,000 yards with up to seven directional changes. The VST requires that the dog follow a track up to five hours old through an urban setting.

FÉDÉRATION CYNOLOGIQUE INTERNATIONALE

Established in 1911, the Fédération Cynologique Internationale (FCI) represents the "world kennel club." This international body brings uniformity to the breeding, judging and showing of pure-bred dogs. Although the FCI originally included only five European nations: France, Germany,

The Anatolian's gait should be powerful yet fluid, demonstrating that the dog is constructed correctly and able to perform the breed's intended function.

Austria, the Netherlands and Belgium (which remains its headquarters), the organization today embraces nations on six continents and recognizes well over 300 breeds of pure-bred dog.

The FCI sponsors both national and international shows. The hosting country determines the judging system and breed standards are always based on the breed's country of origin. Dogs from every country can participate in these impressive canine spectacles, the largest of which is the World Dog Show, hosted in a different country each year.

There are three titles attainable through the FCI: the International Champion, which is the most prestigious; the International Beauty Champion, which is based on aptitude certificates in different countries; and the International Trial Champion, which is based on achievement in obedience trials in different countries. An FCI title requires a dog to win three CACs (*Certificats d'Aptitude au Championnat*) at regional or club shows under three different judges who are breed specialists. The title of International Champion is gained by winning four CACIBs (*Certificats d'Aptitude au Championnat International de Beauté*), which are offered only at international shows, with at least a one-year lapse between the first and fourth award.

The FCI is divided into ten groups, and the Anatolian competes in Group 2 (Molossians). At the World Dog Show, the following classes are offered for each breed: Puppy Class (6–9 months), Junior Class (9–18 months), Open Class (15 months or older) and Champion Class. A dog can be awarded a classification of Excellent, Very Good, Good, Sufficient and Not Sufficient.

SHOW-RING ETIQUETTE

Just as with anything else, there is a certain etiquette to the show ring that can only be learned through experience. Showing your dog can be quite intimidating to you as a novice when it seems as if everyone else knows what he is doing. You can familiarize yourself with ring procedure beforehand by taking showing classes to prepare you and your dog for conformation showing and by talking with experienced handlers. When you are in the ring, it is very important to pay attention and listen to the instructions you are given by the judge about where to move your dog. Remember, even the most skilled handlers had to start somewhere. Keep it up and you too will become a proficient handler as you gain practice and experience.

A GENTLEMAN'S SPORT

Whether or not your dog wins top honors, showing is a pleasant social event. Sometimes, one may meet a troublemaker or nasty exhibitor, but these people should be ignored and forgotten. In the extremely rare case that someone threatens or harasses you or your dog, you can lodge a complaint with the hosting kennel club. This should be done with extreme prudence. Complaints are investigated seriously and should never be filed on a whim.

Puppies can be awarded classifications of Very Promising, Promising or Not Promising. Four placements are made in each class. After all classes are judged, a Best of Breed is selected. Other special groups and classes may also be shown. Each exhibitor showing a dog receives a written evaluation from the judge.

Besides the World Dog Show and other all-breed shows, you can exhibit your dog at specialty shows held by different breed clubs. Specialty shows may have their own regulations.

A post-ring visit to the judges' table, as the handlers get their results...and the dogs look like they're discussing the outcome with each other!

INDEX

My Anatolian Shepherd

PUT YOUR PUPPY'S FIRST PICTURE HERE

Dog's Name _____

Date _____ Photographer _____